Feeling Safe
Confidence for you and your horse

SHADY
Horsemanship

Copyright © Shady Abo Laben, 2017

Contents

Chapter 1 Start feeling safe 5

Chapter 2 The background 9

Chapter 3 The theory.. 21

Chapter 4 Getting ready to start 43

Chapter 5 Catching your horse 71

Chapter 6 Leading your horse 79

Chapter 7 Grooming your horse... 89

Chapter 8 The spooky horse... 101

Chapter 9 Tacking up your horse..................................... 109

Chapter 10 The horse you can't get on 119

Chapter 11 The lazy horse 129

Chapter 12 The horse with no brakes 139

Chapter 13 The horse who won't Load 147

Chapter 14 The horse that bucks 157

Chapter 15 The horse that rears 173

Chapter 16 The horse that bolts...................................... 183

CHAPTER 1
START FEELING SAFE

You're probably looking at this book because you have a problem of some kind with your horse. The chances are you are looking for a sympathetic solution for the two of you: one that makes you both feel confident and safe.

Shady horsemanship is built around being fair to horses, so you have come to the right place.

You must be prepared to be patient, and invest some time and effort. You will be learning a new language – one that you speak with your body – and that takes commitment.

By reading this book you'll learn about:

- The seven pillars that make up the Shady horsemanship method.
- Five exercises that you can perform in-hand and ridden
- How to use the exercises to solve twelve common problems

But most of all you'll learn about communicating with your horse in his language.

How to use this book

You can sit down and read this book from cover to cover, or you can concentrate on your particular problems. If you want to jump about, please read Chapter 3, describing Shady horsemanship theory, and Chapter 4, on getting ready to start, before you go to the chapter about your particular problem.

You might find, though, that your horse's main problem has roots in another problem - maybe your horse bucks because he's lazy and is trying to avoid fast work, for example - so reading all the chapters might widen your horizons and give you more tools and techniques.

Other resources

There are lots of Shady Horsemanship videos online. Watch these to see Shady in action, and to see some moving pictures that might help you refine your own training technique.

https://www.facebook.com/ShadyHorsemanshipUK/

CHAPTER 2
THE BACKGROUND

How can I help people? And why do I want to help them? It's because I was someone who kept horses for a long time without having the right knowledge, and I went through so many problems and difficulties myself, I know what it feels like. When I began to learn a new way of communication, I needed to work on removing my own bad habits. Now when I see a horse and owner not doing well, or having a problem, I can see how I can help both of them.

Normally I work with the owner – so that they can understand their situation better, and learn a different way of dealing with their horse – and I work with the horse – to let the owner see that things **can** be better. The owner needs to believe that if they use the same body language that I'm using, it can work for them too.

My goal in life is to help people understand horses better, and to learn the horse's language so that they can teach their horses anything they need to. I believe that you cannot teach a horse our language; we need to learn their language.

Who is Shady?

You might want to learn a bit more about me before you trust me to help you with your horses, so here is an account of my life story:

Shady has always loved horses, although he came from a non-horsey family in a non-horsey area of his middle-eastern home. As a seven-year old boy he would run outside when he heard the hoofbeats of the only horse in the neighbourhood – driven by an old man in a cart (a reaction more often caused in young boys by the sound of an ice cream van). He kept asking his family to get him a horse, but they weren't rich, had only a patch of back garden, and his father wanted no animals at home. But Shady started saving whatever he could in a money-box. When he reached 12 years old he couldn't wait any longer and entrusted his older brother, Rami, with his savings, demanding 'buy me a horse'.

Shady riding his 'pretend' horse

Rami wanted to help his brother and one day fetched him home from school to present him with a horse! But the horse was an unbroken 3 or 4-year old part-Arab stallion named Adham. Not the ideal mount for a complete beginner! Adham was a strong and dominant horse, and although Shady and Rami worked hard trying to train him, neither of them knew much and there were no good examples in their locality to follow. Unsurprisingly Shady came home injured many times, and stopped counting his falls after 97 (he didn't want to reach the 100). Even when he broke his foot he carried on riding with a plaster cast. At the age of 15 he bought another unbroken horse, this time a thoroughbred mare named Sandy. Somehow Shady survived until the age of eighteen. By then he was not falling off nearly so often, but he still found himself fighting with his horses.

Shady and Adham

the broken foot!

Shady's epiphany came one day when he had a particularly hard time with Adham, who was rearing and biting and striking out. After this confrontation, Shady sat outside the stallion's stable and wept. He admitted to himself that he needed help and took the decision that was to change his *life. He knew there must be a better way of relating to horses, and he knew that there must be someone, somewhere, who could show him what it was. There was no widely available internet back then, so Shady had to start searching the hard way. He asked everyone he knew, and found out that there were such things as riding schools with instructors. There was no way he could afford lessons himself, but twice a week he caught three buses or walked for two hours to watch other people being taught. Then he found a Horsemanship Course advertised in a magazine – one that was designed to produce a horseman who could train horses and teach people. Shady rang and enquired but found that he would have to wait for the following year before there were vacancies, plus he would have to prove that he was qualified to take the course. His heart sank, he knew he was not a 'correct' rider. Uri Peleg – who ran the course – watched Shady ride and commented 'you might be able to stay on a bucking horse, but you know nothing about horses'. Uri must have seen something, however, because he was prepared to let Shady start the course on the condition that he would leave after a month if he showed no improvement.*

Shady found the first two weeks really difficult. Having studied all day he would then go and practice everything on his own horses. Practice, practice, practice. After three weeks, he was given permission to stay on and complete the course. It was the happiest moment of his life! By the end of the course, Shady was addicted to gaining horse knowledge, and just wanted to carry on learning. Back at home he saw the people he used to ride with, and really wanted to make the same change in them that he had experienced. Some listened and some didn't. Shady couldn't afford to set up his own yard then, so started working at other establishments as a new, unknown instructor for pretty low wages. He had to work in the market as well, always needing two jobs at this point. He sometimes ended up working between 12 and 18 hours a day, but he wasn't going to give up his passion for horses.

Shady finally ended up working at a yard in Kfar Makar. There he became more well-known; he gained a reputation for starting horses quickly and with better results, and for turning around problem horses. He taught 80 students a week, mostly children but with some adults. Shady had been working there for nearly a year when they held an open day. Shady showed off a horse he had trained, including bridleless riding, and his students showed off their skills too (including jumping and western riding). At the end of the day a stranger came up to him, looked into his eyes, shook his hand and said 'You can't stop here with your skills and gifts. Go and learn more, and you'll become something really special.' Shady never found out who this stranger was, but he took his comments seriously. That night he took the decision that he would leave his home and travel to the UK. He wanted to know more about the English riding style, and he wanted to learn the language.

While he was working his notice an English-speaking friend found Shady a place at a yard in Hertfordshire where he could start his BHS training. But he would have to start again at the bottom. Shady promised himself that he would not return until he had a certificate, could speak English, had a plan for setting up his own business back home, and, above all, had developed his own method of training.

It was cold, wet and miserable when Shady arrived in England, and he had no warm or waterproof clothing. He had to start at the yard at 7 am the next morning but was totally unprepared and couldn't understand a word anyone was saying. He worked all day mucking out and doing stable jobs with wet feet and wet clothes and no food. He had a one hour lunch break, but didn't know where he could go to eat. The next day was just the same. On the third day he used his electronic translator to tell the yard owner that he was hungry. She took him for a McDonalds breakfast and initiated him into the mysteries of English supermarkets and buses. Unfortunately the yard manager didn't really take to Shady, she told the owner that his lack of English was dangerous and that she should send him back to his own country. In a repeat of his experience with Uri, the owner gave him two weeks to improve. So he started studying English every night, not going to bed until he had memorized 30 or 40 new words. But his electronic translation gadget often led him astray. He made a list of all the objects in the yard in his own language and found a helpful little girl to write the English for each of them as he pointed. So he came to know the all-important words 'broom', 'muck heap', 'wheel-barrow'.

After twelve days the owner called him into her office. Shady's heart was in his mouth, was this the end of his English adventure? She had previously taught him the words 'open' and 'closed' with regards to the door. As he walked in he shut it behind him and with a big grin announced 'door is closed'. This was enough to change the owner's mind about sending him home. She could see that he'd made a big effort and had improved already. Shady stayed for another month, gaining his BHS stage 1 in riding and training (having translated the entire stage 1 manual using his electronic gadget).

While there he met Annette who used to occasionally teach at the yard. She had some problems with her horses at home and was intrigued enough by Shady's 'horsemanship' skills to take him to her yard. Her horse could not pick up the correct canter lead in one direction, and although she was herself an instructor and had had other help, she had been unable to solve the problem. Shady felt the horse's problem, that she was unable to bend in one direction, and started bringing her hindquarters under her more. Within twenty minutes the mare had achieved the elusive canter lead. Her frustrated owner was moved to tears. Believing that she'd seen something special in Shady, Annette started to introduce him to her friends so he could work on their horse problems for them.

Meanwhile Shady moved to work at another yard (living – and freezing – in a caravan). He continued with his BHS training, booking his own exams, and passed the next two stages. In August 2008 he did his first demonstration in the UK, using Annette's horses. He demonstrated bridleless riding on her mare, and took on three other horses to show how his method could work to solve problems of spookiness, laziness, and being difficult to catch. It was a lovely day, and around 80 people attended (at £5 a ticket, it was a bargain).

By September 2009 Shady had his qualifications, he had learned English and had developed his method. He also now had a business plan, so it was time to return to his home country. He opened a yard, the very first time that he *had a horse business of his own. At first there was only him; he had to answer the phone, muck out, teach his clients, feed the horses, and market his business for one whole year all by himself. But the business began to grow, he employed some staff, including additional instructors. It was at this time he acquired the second Sandy as a problem horse (Sandy is the bay quarter horse mare who is nowadays the star of Shady's demonstrations).*

Shady's father had never approved of his son's obsession with horses; he tried to stop Shady's continuing education, believing he wouldn't ever make a living from it. He was positively angry with him when he went to England. But, with the success of Shady's business, for the first time he told his son that he was proud of him.

Shady was renting his yard, and had to move after two years. He moved two more times until he settled in the current premises. (This yard is now run by Shady's brother, Rami, and offers horse therapy, trail rides, and corporate days out, as well as teaching English and Western riding. Shady still returns every year to run horsemanship courses there.)

Sandy

In 2012 Shady decided to start doing demonstrations back in the UK, visiting once or twice a year for two or three weeks at a time. Shady was married by then to a wonderful woman named Neda, and each time he brought her over with him. Shady had decided he would like to move to England, but had to get Neda on board with the idea. At the end of 2014, she agreed to the move. Shady flew his horses, Sandy and Bayan, over in November 2014, and moved himself in early 2015. He took on a yard in Essex and started building a business again. A chance encounter with the owner of Bryerley Springs stables near Milton Keynes gave Shady the chance to move there and take advantage of their two indoor schools and good outriding. Then towards the end of 2016, Shenley Stud in Hertfordshire became vacant, so Shady moved his business to this beautiful, historic stable yard with many acres for turn out, and many more to ride over. He was back very close to where he had started his British equestrian training all those years earlier.

Bayan

Chapter 3
The Theory

Before you start on your training journey with your horse, learning a bit more about the theory behind my method will help prepare you.

One thing I want you to take on board before you start is the importance of separating how you feel about your horse from how you feel about his behaviour. Through my years with horses I came to realise how vital it was to separate my love for these amazing animals from whatever feelings I had about how they had behaved.

When my little son does something that I don't like, I'll go up to him and hug him, then say "Amir, I love you, but I don't like this behaviour". If I couldn't separate my son from his actions, they would become one in my mind and in his mind.

It is similar with horses, but when Amir behaves badly I make him feel uncomfortable by using words, which is a way humans understand but horses don't. With horses you can't give them a hug then explain to them what they've done to upset you. You have to find another way to make them feel uncomfortable, but you must remain calm and relaxed, and still love the animal the same amount as you did before he behaved badly. You will have a much better result if you act in this way.

Above all else, I want you to be fair to your horses. To help with this I have a framework based on seven pillars. Give this a quick read through now, but, more importantly, refer back to it when you start working through the rest of the book.

The language of horses

The first of the seven pillars is horse language. It's about learning how horses communicate with one another and then using that knowledge. We can use our own version of horse language to communicate with them both from the ground and in the saddle.

Pressure and release are at the very heart of the language. There are three types of pressure used by horses when they communicate with each other: voice pressure, sign pressure and physical pressure.

Voice pressure

Horse don't really use voice pressure an awful lot. If you think about it, horses are usually silent. You are most likely to hear them when they are anxiously calling after a friend who has been taken away from them, or you might hear them nicker to welcome the friend back, or to greet their food bucket. If they are happy and relaxed they might blow through their lips. If they are scared of something and perceive danger they might snort. They might squeal when they meet a new horse or a rival. But on the whole, if everything is fine in a horse's world, they're quiet. Horses easily learn to ignore sound. They live in a noisy world and they screen out much of what they hear and regard it as a 'nothing'.

Shady's 7 Pillars

Horse Jumping	Cross Country	Western Riding	Hacking	Dressage	Ground Work
Language	Method & Technique	Self-Awareness	Read Horses	10 Exercises	Plan	Signs

Sign pressure

Sign pressure is making some movement but without physical contact. Think how a simple flick of an ear from a dominant horse can have another horse backing away pretty fast. The use of signs is very obvious if you watch the communication between a mother and a foal. She can use the swishing of her tail to move a foal on, or turn him towards her. Like voice pressure, however, the horse can often ignore sign pressure. Both pressures can be screened out to become a 'nothing' after about three seconds. A mother might try to move her foal to one side by gesturing with her nose. If she doesn't get a response within a couple of seconds, she will move to physical pressure.

Physical pressure

Physical pressure is probably the most obvious to observe between horses, like the mother pushing her foal's nose with her nose to move him to one side. But it is not all about giving an order to a foal, or a bite or a kick, and aggression. Horses also communicate using physical contact in many pleasant ways. They are playful animals, and might nip each other on the back end as part of this play. Horses love mutual grooming sessions with a trusted friend, and they particularly like having their withers 'done'. It is a good test of your relationship with your horse to try to rub their withers yourself. If they relax and enjoy it, you are also identified as a 'trusted friend', if they are wary then you have some work to do to improve your relationship, if they raise their heads, and try to move away from you then your relationship needs serious attention!

Horse language is the first pillar of my method because the tools used are all based on this language. When you ask a horse to do something you will start with a voice or a sign pressure, but if the horse ignores that then you can escalate to using physical pressure. You always start using this language from the ground. Horses don't get on each other to give instructions (in fact, in nature it is predators that would leap on their backs), so you should always start learning their language while you are on your feet, not theirs.

Methods and techniques

The methods and techniques, most simply put, are the tools that you use to communicate with your horse.

Psychology balance

This is a phrase you'll come across often in this book, and it needs some explanation. Psychology balance is about swapping around your horse's expectation of things so that he cannot always predict what you're going to ask next. If he cannot predict, then he will wait for you to instruct him. Psychology balance is also about you working out what your horse needs or wants at any one time and finding a way of giving him it that suits both of you.

Here is an example of how psychology balance might work in your everyday riding life. Say you often ride your horse in an arena and you usually finish your session in the middle. But now you find that he's always trying to come into the middle of the arena. How can you change this? You have to change his expectation of what the middle of the arena means, but first you must understand why your horse is doing this. He is seeking safety and comfort, and you won't solve the problem by saying 'no, you can't have what you want', you will solve it by showing him that he can have safety and comfort in other places, but that he has to wait to be told when and where. In this situation you could change his expectations by choosing to let him rest at different places in the arena at different times during your schooling session. You could give him a break next to a jump, then maybe back in the middle of the arena, even by the arena entrance.

Here's another example. When you come back from a hack, your horse is probably anticipating going back to his stable or field and being with his friends, and he might not be listening to you. You could try leaving fifteen minutes at the end of the ride to turn round again just before you get home, or ride him back into the yard and out again a few times. If he does this without any objection, it shows that he is happily waiting for your instructions, otherwise you need to repeat these exercises to stop him anticipating.

You need to incorporate psychology balance into handling your horse as well as riding him. You can start with everyday things like turning out, picking up feet, feeding. Do you have issues with worming your horse? Get hold of a big plastic syringe (you can get these from farming suppliers). Fill it full of something sweet that your horse will enjoy, like pureed apple. For the three days before you are due to worm him, feed him the treat from the syringe. That should change his whole expectation of what happens when you put a syringe in his mouth.

Does your horse always pull you over to a nice fresh patch of grass when you try to lead him through a field? Try turning him back and starting again every time he stops to eat (this probably works better to start with when you are turning him out rather than bringing him in). But it is quite natural for a horse to want to eat grass, and you do want to meet his needs, so when he is being good and walking with you, select a particularly tasty looking patch, and stop and invite him to graze for a minute or so. Again you are mixing up his expectations, but encouraging him to always listen to you for instructions.

You might have been told numerous times that horses love routine, and a lot of psychology balance is about deliberately disrupting routine, so how does this work? I believe that horses are happier when they don't know what to expect. For example, horses that get fed or turned out at exactly the same time every day can get very anxious. They will often bang the stable door or start box walking when the magic time approaches. A horse that can accept his routine being changed, and will trust you to meet his requirements somehow, is much less stressed. Mix up your management; you need to have a plan but you also need to be able to change it. A happy horse is a relaxed horse, and one that is much less likely to injure himself when he is turned out into the field.

Physical Balance

Physical balance means that a horse is equally able to do things on either side. This means he should trot a twenty metre circle to the right as well as he can trot a twenty metre circle to the left. He should move laterally the same each way, move his hindquarters the same each way, bend the same each way.

If your horse is not balanced, you need to find out why. You should take care to rule out any health-related reasons. Have his back checked, his saddle, and his teeth. Problems with any of these could be physically preventing him from being balanced.

But it could have an entirely psychological cause. It may be that some conflict has made him resistant on one side. It might be that he is stiffer on one side – he finds it harder to move that way, although it is not causing him actual pain. In either of these cases, you can use your psychology balance tools to overcome these problems.

Say your horse flatly refuses to canter on the left lead. Whether you are lunging him or riding him, he resists. Start cantering him on a right circle, the direction he is happy with and feels balanced, then stop and change rein and **walk** him to the left. Repeat this, keeping the balance between cantering on the right rein and walking on the left rein. He should start to feel happy to go left because he's getting a rest there. Then you can start asking for a little more: ask him to trot on the left rein, but keep the balance between the two directions. When you work up to cantering on the bad lead, do it right at the end of the session and keep it short. For example, repeat cantering one circle to the right then one circle to the left two or three times. Then end for the day. Repeat this for about three days. You should now be getting the same good result on each rein, and when you have this established, repeat for another three days.

You can use this balancing method for all sorts of physical imbalances. The important thing is to start by making moving to the bad side easy and a place of relief, while the harder work is happening in their 'favourite' direction.

The 7/7/7 formula

One of the key techniques that you'll be learning is called '7/7/7'. So what is that? It's about how often you need to repeat something, and for how long, to be sure that the horse has really learned it. Basically it means that you repeat an exercise so that you have seven good times, over seven good days, and then give the horse seven breaks during which you don't do the exercise. When you try again, your horse picks it up again straight away. Once you have achieved the 7/7/7, you can go to a maintenance level and just repeat the exercise every so often.

The 7/7/7 formula applies to all exercises, ridden or on the ground. An exercise in this context can be an activity like backing up to your command using rope/halter/stick, but it can also be something more general like loading into a trailer, passing a scary object, or even achieving a certain quality of canter.

The 7/7/7 formula was arrived at after years of training horses (and making many mistakes!). I came to recognise that not every horse is the same; some need more repetition to learn things, some need less. But I found that, although not every horse might need 7/7/7 to learn something (clever horses with good memories might be able to learn using a 3/3/3 formula), you are just about guaranteed to teach any horse if you stick to using 7/7/7.

In the problem chapters I often talk about 'when you've had three good times in a row over three good days'. That is really the minimum repetition, you should probably read it as 'three to seven, depending on your horse's personality'.

Being consistent in your training is important. You don't expect your children, or even yourself, to be able to memorize something instantly, so why would you expect your horse to do it? Say your friend got a new phone number, you couldn't read it just once then expect to recall it the next day. If you rang your friend every day for a week, you probably wouldn't need to look the number up. But if you then didn't call them for a month, you would likely have forgotten the number and would need to look it up again.

If you use the 7/7/7 formula when teaching your horse an exercise, you can assess how quick a learner he is, and how good a memory he has. These are not exactly the same thing. Some horses learn really quickly, but seem to forget really quickly too. Others might seem to take an age to 'get' something, but once they have 'got' it, it stays there. Remember that ALL horses are intelligent and ALL horses have memory, it's just that some will require more patience from you, and some less.

This diagram shows how the 7 good exercises over 7 good days might work. Note that the seven good exercises must be consecutive (i.e. seven in a row), but the good days do not **have** to be consecutive. If you are working with a horse with a particularly bad memory, then consecutive days will help, however.

Mon	✗ ✗ ✗ ✓ ✗ ✗ ✓ ✓ ✓ ✗ ✓ ✓ ✓ ✗ ✓ ✓ ✓ ✗ ✓ ✓ ✓ ✓ ✓ ✓ ✓ — 7 good times!	Mon	day off
Tues	✗ ✓ ✗ ✓ ✓ ✓ ✓ ✓ ✓ — 7 good times!	Tues	✗ ✓ ✓ ✓ ✓ ✓ ✓ ✓ — 7 good times!
Weds	day off	Weds	day off
Thurs	✓ ✗ ✓ ✓ ✓ ✓ ✓ ✓ ✓ — 7 good times!	Thurs	✓ ✓ ✓ ✓ ✓ ✓ ✓ — 7th good day, 7 good times!
Fri	day off	Fri	day off
Sat	✓ ✓ ✓ ✓ ✓ ✓ ✓ — 7 good times!	Sat	day off
Sun	✓ ✓ ✓ ✓ ✓ ✓ ✓ — 7 good times!	Sun	day off

When you've completed this part you'll have a pretty good idea how quickly your horse learns something new. The next part is to work out how well they remember it, and this is where the seven breaks come in. The next diagram shows how you might build in seven breaks across a 4-week period. In this example you can see that the horse is remembering the exercise pretty well when the breaks are lasting up to five days. With some exercises and some horses, your breaks could last a week or more.

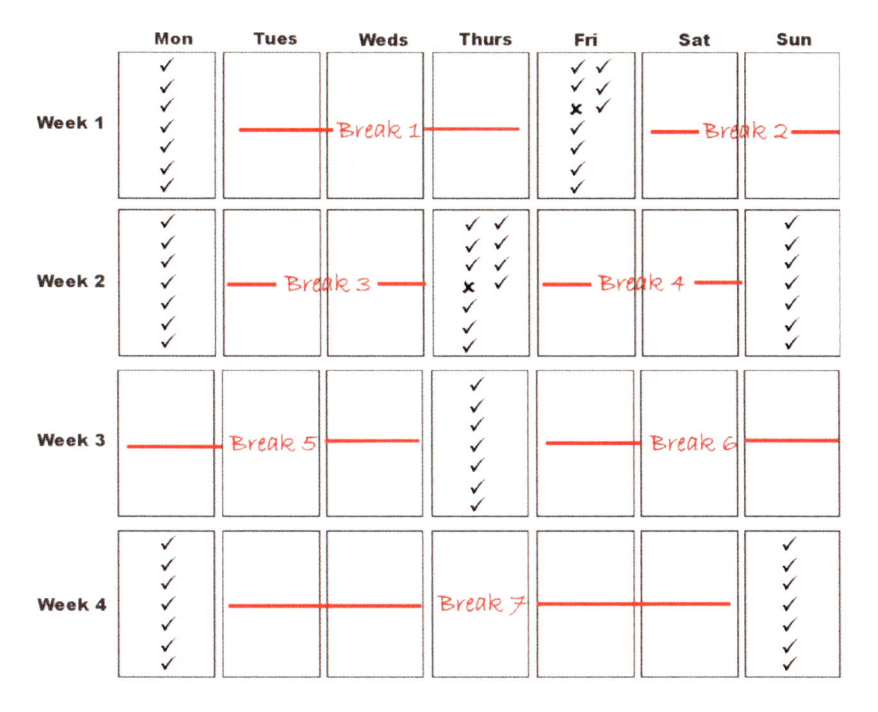

	Mon	Tues	Weds	Thurs	Fri	Sat	Sun
Week 1	✓✓✓✓✓✓✓	—— Break 1 ——————			✓✓ ✓✓ x✓ ✓ ✓ ✓	—— Break 2 ——	
Week 2	✓✓✓✓✓✓✓	—— Break 3 ——		✓✓ ✓✓ ✓✓ x✓ ✓ ✓ ✓	—— Break 4 ——		✓✓✓✓✓✓✓
Week 3		—— Break 5 ——		✓✓✓✓✓✓✓	—— Break 6 ——		
Week 4	✓✓✓✓✓✓✓			—— Break 7 ——			✓✓✓✓✓✓✓

After you have successfully completed the 7/7/7 formula with a particular exercise you can think about going onto a maintenance regime. You need to give your horse fairly regular reminders of something new that they have learned. This helps to maintain quality or confidence (depending on what you have taught them). How often do you need to repeat? Once a week? Once every two weeks? Once a month? Again, this will largely depend on your horse, and you will need to experiment to find out what's best for him. It also depends on what you've been teaching. For example, if you've been teaching your horse to overcome some fear or recover from some trauma it might well take a year to work out the correct maintenance schedule. Say your horse has had a long-standing loading problem, you might need to load and travel him once or twice a month for the next two or three years before you can really proclaim that he is 'fixed' (it is a journey in more ways than one!)

If you are working with problems of fear or confidence you can take extra steps to help yourself succeed. Imagine your horse is scared of sheep, and you are using your 7/7/7 formula to ride him past a nearby field currently full of ewes and lambs. Before you start the exercises, spend some time in the school with him to make sure he is listening to you. This will build his confidence – and yours. Don't put yourself under unnecessary pressure, either. Say that you have entered a competition on the weekend and it's really important that your horse loads and doesn't make you late. Do not leave it until the morning of your show, and hope that your training has worked. Even if you have successfully completed the 7/7/7 formula and are in 'maintenance' mode, make sure you practice loading your horse for the three days before. This will help both of you be in the right frame of mind when it's important that he gets in.

Self-awareness

This means being aware of yourself and what you are doing. Generally you should aim for being as still as possible, whether you are training from the ground or in the saddle. Then make all of your movements meaningful. Be aware of:

- What you want
- When you want it
- How you want it

- What you need to do to get that result

Take notice of your own body language. Make all of you movements mean something, so that you don't teach your horse to ignore your body language. Be particularly conscious of exactly where you are adding pressure.

Make sure that, in your training, you move your horse and your horse doesn't move you. For example, when you're leading your horse from the side as a training exercise, ensure that he moves off first as a response to your aids. As a leader you should build on how much your movement and your body language means to your horse. If you move all the time, then your movement becomes a 'nothing' to your horse, and he will feel that he can safely ignore you.

It is also important that your horse is not scared by your body language. Your aim is to have him watching you in a calm manner and working out from your movement whether you want something or nothing from him.

If you really work on awareness of every movement of every bit of you, then you can get to the point where your horse can pick up small changes in your intention, and take these as commands. This becomes the 'A' pressure that is described in the next chapter. Use this same 'A' pressure again and again until the horse understands.

Reading horses

As a horse owner or trainer you must know the basics of reading horses. You have to know when your horse is scared of something, recognise what type of fear it is, and have some idea of what caused it. You should also know when your horse is confused and be able to tell the difference between a horse being dominant, and not wanting to do something, and a horse being confused and not understanding what to do. You need to distinguish between a horse who is protecting himself, and a horse who is testing you. When you are training, you should be able to recognise when a horse has understood what you are asking of him. A horse will often show that he's got the message by making licking and chewing motions. Horses tend to lick and chew as a sign that they are relaxing after some tension and anxiety that they've experienced.

The main things that all horses seek in their life are safety and comfort. If you develop your skills at reading your horse and help him, through your training, to feel safe and comfortable then, to him, you are the best owner in the world!

The ten exercises

The ten exercises are the foundation of the Shady Horsemanship courses. The exercises are performed both in-hand and ridden.

In this book you will be learning a subset of these exercises to help you deal with common problems you might be struggling with with your horse.

The ten exercises are:

1. Something and nothing

2. Back up

3. Move the front end, move the back end

4. Lead your horse while positioned in all different zones

5. Snaking around and having your horse following the reins.

6. Move back and forth through narrow spaces

7. Move sideways

8. 'Read my mind' exercises

9. Work on a circle

10. Perform transitions

This book starts you on the course of learning the ten exercises, and more detailed descriptions of the ones you will use are given in the next chapter.

Planning

Many owners (and even trainers) have no plan whatsoever when they set about training their horse. Instead, they have a set of goals, and they concentrate on these goals rather than on the journey that might help them reach them.

Having a plan and putting it together includes considering your horse's ability, personality, memory and intelligence, and being realistic about how many times a week you will be able to train your horse. You should also incorporate psychology balance into the plan to build your horse's confidence.

It is important to take your journey at your horse's speed, do not overface him. If someone can't even tie their horse up in the yard, they shouldn't expect to take him to a strange place to compete, just because it's one of their goals. They might get away with it if they keep the horse busy, but if he misbehaves, they will probably blame him, and he will get a bad reputation.

Having a plan is like having a recipe for a new dish that you want to cook. It means that you have got the right ingredients to hand, and you'll have some guidance on what to do with them to achieve a good result.

There is an example training plan in the next chapter, which should give you some ideas on how to make your own plans.

The signs

The signs are what help you recognise if you are on the right path with the right training plan. The signs are built on the expectation of the results of your plan. Every plan should aim at getting a particular result, with a sign you are looking for to show that you have achieved it.

As an analogy if you multiply 5 by 5, you expect to get the result 25. The number 25 is your sign, if you get 21 instead, it means something is wrong.

For example, say that you have a plan this week to teach your horse to move sideways in hand with you standing in front of him. At the end of the week, your horse is moving sideways, but you notice that, as you're moving him sideways, he's pushing you backwards. You start positioned in the middle of the arena but when you finish you're standing near one end. This is a sign that you should work on your horse's backing up more, because at the moment he's not respecting pressure on the halter.

When you've improved your back up, you might go back to the sideways training and find you're not driven backwards. That's good, but now you notice that his back end is turning towards you as he moves, so he's at a slant. Now you can refine your training plan to work on your control of his back end, so that your horse keeps straight as he moves sideways.

Reading the signs and revisiting your training plan should become a routine that you spend 30 minutes or so on every week.

That brings us to the end of the seven pillars, but there's another idea I want to share with you before you start on your training journey.

Home

I always like to make sure that a horse has somewhere to go back to when anything goes wrong in the training. Maybe the horse is scared of something, or is getting dominant or confused, so we need a place to go back to to restart the training. This is the home area. For a horse it is the place where they know that they are safe and nothing is going to hurt them (just like we should feel when we get home).

There are two home areas – one when you are on the ground, and one when you are in the saddle.

On the ground, whenever your horse comes towards you and stands still next to you, he should know that this is the safe area. He should never feel sorry for coming back to you. No matter what he has just done, or how he has just behaved, you have to welcome your horse back. The worst thing that can happen with your relationship is that he starts to think twice about coming to you in case you hurt him. Imagine yourself as a child, you've got into trouble and are feeling really scared, but when you get home your mum or dad are waiting for you and hurt you and tell you off in the worst possible way. The next time you do something wrong you will try to go to somewhere else instead of going back to your home. It doesn't feel like home anymore: it's no longer a place of peace and safety.

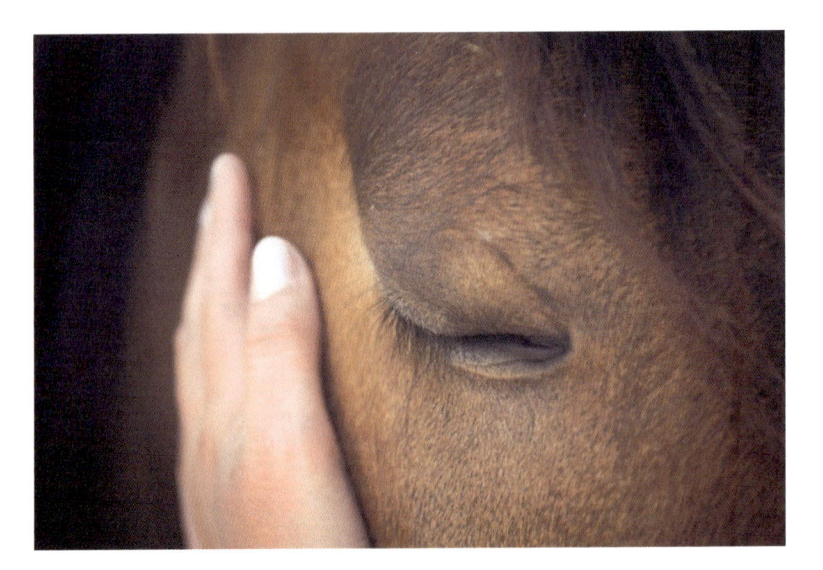

In the saddle, whenever your horse stops, he should feel 100% certain that you will not hurt him. He should be able to stop if he is not sure, and have that as a 'home'. Even if your horse is lazy and stops when you don't want him to, you must be careful not to get angry with him. Yes, you can ask him to move forward again by putting pressure on and releasing when he moves, but maybe give him a safety and comfort moment after a few strides (you do have to be careful to maintain the home zone without making a lazy horse lazier).

Chapter 4
Getting Ready to Start

Above everything else, I want to teach you how to be fair with horses. Here is a list of the most important things to know if you want to be fair:

1. Start looking for how you can learn to speak the horse's language; when you do this you are already doing a lot to be fair to your horse. Think about how you speak English fluently, but I couldn't speak it at all. I had to learn English to be able to communicate with you, and so I have already done a lot for our relationship!

2. Make an effort to find out what horses look for, what they like to do, and what they don't. Take time to work out what are their biggest worries in life, and how you can take care of this for them.

3. Work on absorbing and understanding the information in Chapter 3 before you actually start working with your horse.

4. Have a plan of what you are going to be doing and how, and also have a plan B in case you need it.

5. Do your best to be as clear as possible with your pressure and release, and remember that horses learn from the release and the comfort.

6. Work for tomorrow. That means when you have a good result stop there, and the next day maybe do some more.

7. Cover your future. For example, if you know that you are going to ride with other horses and that they may leave you, practice with some friend before. If you know you are going to ride in a place where there are lorries or tractors around, check that your horse is good with heavy traffic first. If our horses are scared of something, normally this is because we didn't prepare them for it.

There are many other things that we can do to be more fair to our horses, but I have found that for everything we have the minimum and the basics, and the seven points above are the really important ones.

What is your problem?

Before you start working on any problems with the help of this book, ask yourself these questions (take your time thinking about your answers, and maybe write them down somewhere):

1. What exactly is the problem? Be as detailed as you can in your answer. For example, rather than just writing 'difficult to load', write a description of exactly what happens when you try to load your horse. Maybe he will put his front feet on the ramp, and then just refuse to budge another inch? Maybe as soon as you get within six feet of the trailer, he rears up, or tries to spin and run away?

2. When did your problems begin? For example, did your horse used to be easy to catch, but is now really difficult? When did you notice the change, did it happen suddenly or gradually get worse over time?

3. Is your horse showing any signs of fear when he misbehaves? This might include lifting his head, his eyes becoming wide and showing more of the white, and becoming tense in his body.

4. What is your horse looking for when he acts like that? For example, is he refusing to load because he seeks comfort and safety and your trailer does not offer either of these feelings for him.

Here's an example of a problem someone has written up:

1. My horse is OK most of the time, but then something happens to make him anxious, and he becomes really reactive. In the worst case, encountering a thing that he's normally OK with makes him totally freak, and he turns tail and heads for home. He's very hard to stop and it really puts me off riding him.

2. He was OK for the first year I owned him, but then something went wrong and I had several bolting incidents. He will go for months feeling fine, but then something happens (I don't always know what) and he just loses his confidence.

3. When he loses confidence he can be harder to catch, and he is very anxious and fidgety when brought into the yard. He is hyper-vigilant about sights and sounds.

4. I don't think he likes feeling like that. He is seeking safety, and probably most wants to be back in the field with his friends.

One of the great things about the methods that you are going to learn is that you can practice them without the horse. Try out the exercises with a human friend acting the part of the horse (whether they are a nice horse or a naughty horse is up to them!).

Playing the horse role

Before you move on to working with a real horse, please consider these points:

- Always keep yourself safe. If you aren't sure about something, don't just plough on regardless. Read the instructions again, and don't start until you feel more certain about what you're doing.

- When you do decide to start, don't dither. Be confident that you can carry on and see the exercise through.

Pressure and release are at the very heart of the methods you are going to use to communicate with your horse.

there are three types of pressure used by
n they communicate with each other:

e pressure (horses don't really use this all that
h)

- Sign pressure (much more popular with horses)
- Physical pressure (the most commonly used by horses)

You are going to learn to classify the pressures that you use when working with your horse as being A pressure, B, C or D pressure.

A pressure is always your first choice. It is a sign or a voice command, or the softest of physical pressures. The A pressure is what you want your horse to respond to after you have trained him.

B pressure is when you start with physical pressure (or add a bit more force to the soft physical pressure that you are already using).

C pressure is adding yet more physical pressure if your horse does not respond to B. You normally should not go past this pressure with your horse, and after you have been training for a while, A or B would normally be enough.

D pressure is the pressure that you hide in your pocket, and only use when you really have to. Don't use this when you are angry or exasperated; rather view its use as a way of saying to your horse 'look, I have more power, please don't make me use it'. In this way you are only using the D pressure as a way to give your horse more reasons for doing something for you.

You must always be careful when using pressure with your horse and, as you might expect, there are some rules to observe:

1. Don't start until you are ready! Be standing in the right place, with the right equipment. Know exactly what you want, where to aim your pressure, and what the result should look like.

2. Once you have started, don't stop until you get a result (even if it's only a small result).

3. Always start with an A pressure.

4. Never go up to a pressure that you cannot physically maintain.

5. When you have the result you aimed for, release the pressure. Either stop altogether, or go back to the A pressure if you want the horse to continue.

Equipment

You do not need a lot of expensive equipment to use the methods described in this book. You don't have to have an arena either, any area that you can set aside for training will do.

If you need just one thing, it's a string halter and a long rope (12 feet or 3.6 metres). Next you might get a horsemanship stick (the 4ft stick with a string attached). Next most important is a saddle and a bridle. After that a 'nice to have' is a couple of 23 ft (7 metre) long reins (a couple of lunge lines would do this job), and a pair of spurs.

That's it!

It all depends on the way you use your equipment. I'm not violently opposed to other gadgets such as martingales or side reins, but they don't really help a horse to learn, they just physically restrain him.

All your equipment should be there to help you and your horse have better communication, to help you with your timing of pressure and release, and to improve your body movement. The less you move, the better it is, and the recommended equipment will help you with this.

Before you use any equipment to put pressure on a horse, make sure that your horse is happy with that equipment. For example, you should not use the horsemanship stick on a horse if he is frightened of it. You'd need to work on getting him happy with it before you could use it for training (see 'something and nothing' a bit later in this chapter). It's a good idea to practice your stick technique away from your horse; you don't want to end up hitting your horse with it when you mean to stroke him. The stick acts like an extension to your arm and enables you to stand still in one spot. It is especially useful in helping you reach his hindquarters.

Use the softest bit that you can with your horse. As your training progresses, you should aim to switch to a gentler bit. For example, if you are currently using a Dutch gag, when you feel your horse is softer in the mouth and has learned to react to your pressure, after a good seven days you can fix your reins to gentler part of the bit. Aim to eventually swap to a snaffle.

Be prepared to abandon tight nosebands too. Dropped nosebands, flashes, grackles and so on are designed to stop your horse opening his mouth. He opens his mouth to avoid pressure. As your training progresses and your horse learns that you release pressure when he obeys, then you should be able to swap to a loose noseband, or no noseband at all.

You might be surprised that I have listed spurs in the required equipment. They have quite a bad reputation, but, used correctly, they can be kinder to a horse. Spurs enable a rider to apply an aid with better timing. You can use the spurs gently while maintaining a quiet position in the saddle. Just kick, kick, kicking at the side of a horse can do more damage than the spurs, even though it is damage that you cannot actually see.

Using your equipment

If any of the equipment doesn't improve your relationship with your horse, the chances are you're not using it correctly. Used properly, all the equipment should improve your timing and your body language, and improve the 'next time' response that you get from your horse.

With any equipment, never ever use it in anger. Never ask your horse to do anything when you have lost your temper. If you are angry, you need to walk away and deal with your issues before you approach your horse again. The end result that you are looking for is a horse that is obedient because he understands what you are asking him, not because he is frightened of you.

A common problem is to give the release part of the 'pressure and release' at the wrong time. This is why it's important not to put on more pressure than you can maintain. Be prepared to keep up the pressure for a long time if you're getting no response, but in this situation, as soon as you get any response, you must release.

Patience is everything, don't be afraid to keep on going with your pressure, whoever might be watching. You can always outwait your horse, and if you are in a hurry your energy is all wrong. Be happy to stay where you are, keeping the pressure up, and behave as if you have all the time in the world. You have to believe that the horse will not ignore you forever, he will eventually do something about the pressure.

The basic exercises

Before you start on the 'problem solving' chapters, familiarise yourself with these exercises, because they are the ones that you will be using to resolve particular problems. You can refer back to this section as you start working on the problems.

Something and nothing

A horse divides everything he experiences into either a **something** or a **nothing**. A **something** has to be paid attention to – it is a stimulus that provokes some response. The **something** could be a bad thing or a good thing, and the response to it might be one that we are pleased to get, or one that we definitely don't want.

The **nothing** for a horse is a stimulus that can safely be ignored; the horse knows he doesn't have to waste precious energy responding to it. But it might be a stimulus that we want them to attend to.

The 2 Sides Of A Horse Brain

Something — Nothing

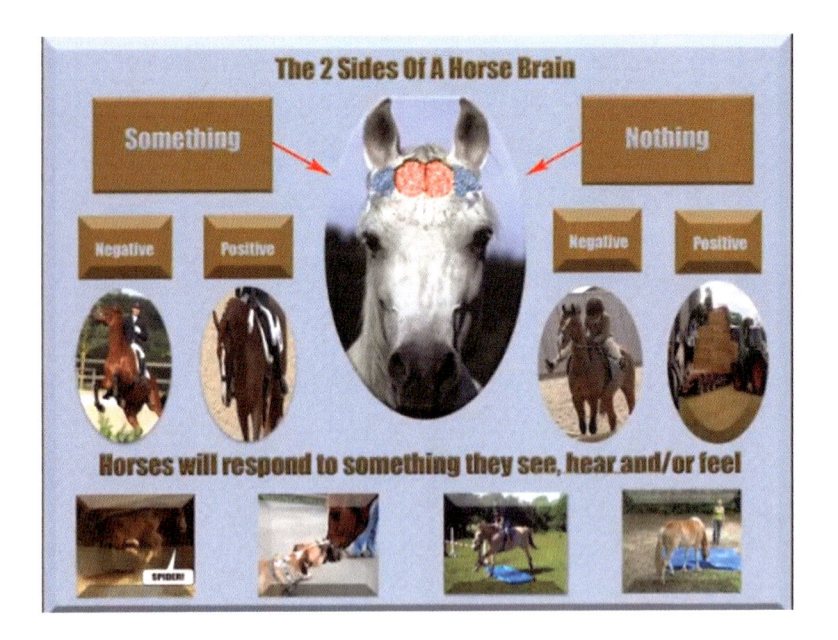

Negative — Positive — Negative — Positive

Horses will respond to something they see, hear and/or feel

A lot of horse training is about matching up our idea of something and nothing with their idea of something and nothing.

Imagine that you are out for a hack with your horse. There's a discarded carrier bag caught on a hedge and flapping about. You want your horse to regard that as a nothing, but to your horse it's a big scary something. Later on you want to ride past a lane that is a shortcut back to the yard. Your horse wants to turn for home, you want to carry on and enjoy a longer ride. You squeeze his sides, which should be a something to him, but it's a nothing in his mind, and you end up kicking him, and hitting him with a whip to get him to agree about the route you're going to ride.

So how can you go about training your horse to agree with your views on somethings and nothings, so that you are both reading from the same script? You can make a start with exercises on the ground, using a horsemanship stick and a string. Don't think of the stick as a 'whip', a punishment device; think of it as an extension to your arm, a way of touching your horse from a distance. The aim of the exercise initially is to get your horse to regard your actions with the stick as a nothing, actions that he ignores and feels relaxed about. He should learn to take his lead from you – you are telling him it's nothing, and he trusts you and he is happy to accept your opinion.

Stand facing your horse, holding onto the rope loosely in your left hand. With the stick and string both held in your right hand (so that the string is not flapping loose) gently rub the stick over your horse's neck and shoulders. You should be as relaxed as possible – breathe deeply and drop your shoulders. What you do next depends on how your horse reacts.

If he is calm and relaxed and happy with this experience, you can progress. Stand to one side and rub the stick over his back and quarters. If he is still happy and accepting with this contact, progress to rubbing under his belly, and down his back legs. If you get to this stage, swap hands so that his rope is in your right hand and the stick in your left. Repeat the process on his other side. (He might be more reactive on his right side because most of us lead and mount from his left side.)

If at any point your horse reacts negatively to being stroked with the stick, just gently persist until he relaxes and accepts this contact as a nothing. Even if this means you spend the whole session just rubbing his left shoulder, watch for him relaxing and accepting (he might start a chewing motion).

If things are going well with the rubbing, go back to having the rope in your left hand and the stick in your right. Let go of the string, so that your stick now looks more like a lunge whip. Gently lay the string over the horse's withers. If he accepts that, stroke his back with the string, and progress so that you can drape it all over him. Again, change your hands around and repeat the exercise on the other side.

It might take you several sessions to get to the stage where you can rub your horse with stick, and then string, all over on both sides. Remember, the aim of the exercise is to get your horse to accept an experience that was previously a something as now being a nothing, based on your guidance.

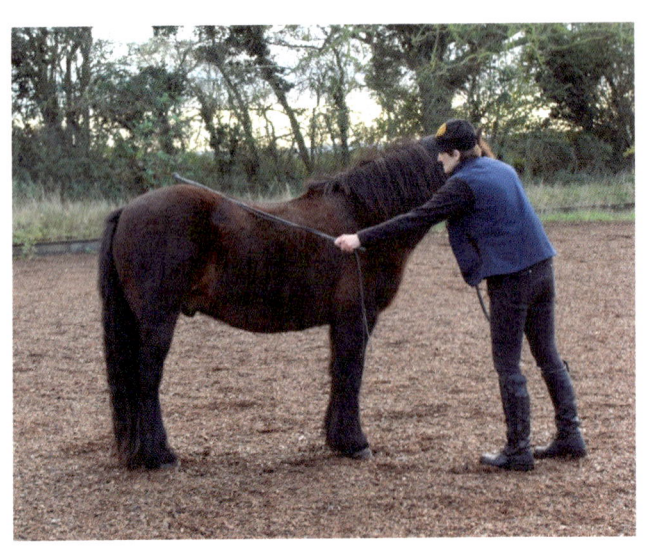

touching with the stick

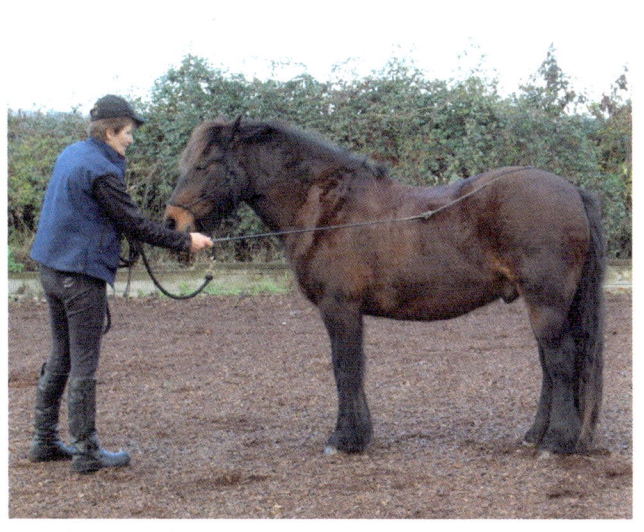

touching with the string

From then on, always start any in hand training sessions with a 'something and nothing' exercise.

Backing up

Backing up in reaction to your pressure is a crucial lesson both when working in hand and when in the saddle. You use backing up to get your horse responsive both to the halter on his nose, and to the bit in his mouth.

To back up in-hand, you are aiming to use the rope to put pressure on the horse's nose through the halter. The horse backs away in response to that pressure. Hold the rope around half a metre from the clip with your arm bent at the elbow. An 'A' pressure in this context is to just pull on the rope in a soft rhythm, by flicking your wrist. It is the weight of the rope more than anything that should put the pressure on the horse's nose. If you have to use more pressure, move your arm up and down, but be careful not to take your arm behind you, and always move back to the starting position with each shake of the rope.

As soon as your horse takes a step back, release the pressure. Then aim to use an 'A' pressure to maintain backward movement, but increase the pressure if your horse isn't listening. If your horse is really resisting, rather than increasing the rope pressure to a level that you can't maintain, tap the horse on his chest with your stick while you continue to use the rope.

backing up

You also need to master another variant of the backing up exercise, with you standing still, while the horse backs away from you until he's standing at the extent of the rope. Start by facing your horse, holding the end of your rope, with the rest of it resting on the ground between you and your horse. Start gently agitating the rope up and down in a sort of snaking motion. That should put enough weight on the nose of the halter to make your horse back up. (You can shake the rope from side to side if you prefer). Take the pressure off when he is standing about 10 feet away from you. Let him stand still for a while, then bring him back towards you.

backing up – the second method

To back the horse up from the saddle, take your legs away from his side, and simply pull on the reins. The aim is to get him to move away from the pressure in his mouth, just as he's learned to move away from the pressure on his nose when you taught him the exercise on the ground.

With backing up in-hand or in the saddle, do not use more pressure than you can maintain. The key is to keep the pressure up until the horse responds. Remember that you can outwait him!

Moving the front end and the back end

Being able to get your horse to move his front legs away from you (a turn on the haunches) and move his back legs away from you (a turn on the forehand) is a useful skill in all sort of circumstances. You should only do this exercise after you have got your horse to be happy with the stick touching and rubbing his nose.

Start by moving the front end. Stand at your horses left shoulder, holding the rope in your left hand and the stick and string with your right (you can reverse hands if you like). Gently wave the stick at his nose to encourage him to move it away from you. You want his front legs to follow his nose, crossing over as they move, while the back legs hardly move at all. Some horses respond better to pressure on their necks or their shoulders rather than their noses. Horses need to take their weight back to do this movement, and might get 'stuck' moving their shoulders. You might have to increase the pressure to tapping with the stick to get a result. Release and rub with the stick when he has moved his front end. Repeat the exercise standing at his right shoulder, holding the rope in your right hand and the stick and string in your left.

moving the front end

To move his back end, start by standing just behind his left fore with your left leg by his girth line, facing backwards. Hold the rope in your left hand, and the stick and string in your right. Start gently waving the stick at his quarters until he steps his back legs away from you (you might need to tap his quarters if he doesn't respond within three seconds). He might need to cross his back legs to enable him to step round. He should not step forward. When he has moved round, release and rub, then repeat the exercise on the other side.

moving the back end

Leading from the side

This might sound a bit simplistic, surely everyone can lead their horse from the side? But this is the technique of leading a horse without him pushing or barging or pulling forwards or backwards. It is a foundation skill of you controlling his go and his slow. You should also be able to back him up from this position. Being able to lead is such an important part of your relationship, that a whole chapter is devoted to it. If your horse is at all rude when led, you need to read that chapter as well as this summary.

leading from the side

Stand by your horses shoulder with the rope in the hand nearest him and the stick in the hand further away. Hold the rope quite loosely, so that there is a loop between your hand and the clip. Let the long end of the rope drag along the floor next to him (most horses get used to this very quickly and it is a good lesson for them to learn, but prepare your horse by making sure he won't panic if the rope touches his legs). You want to put pressure on your horse so that he starts walking first. Begin by just leaning forward as if you're about to take a step, if he doesn't move within two seconds start describing a small circle with your stick (almost like rowing a boat). If that is not enough pressure, be a bit more vigorous, so that the string makes a noise as it hits the ground. If that is still not enough, touch the horse's quarters with the string in the same rhythm until he moves.

Keep walking around, staying by your horse's shoulder. If your horse moves his nose and starts to drift inwards, quickly change your grip on the stick so that you are holding the end where the string attaches, and just wave it at his nose with the handle end to straighten him up (you might need to tap if he doesn't listen).

Work on getting him to stop when you stop. If he walks on with you standing there, shake the rope to make him stop and back up until his shoulder is level to where you are standing. Also work on making him back up further, agitate the rope and have him walks backwards with you for ten or so steps.

To change direction, you should just turn on your heel, swapping over the rope and the stick as you turn. Your horse should turn and rearrange himself so that he is facing in the opposite direction and you are standing by his other shoulder (the horse shouldn't walk around you).

Moving sideways

Moving your horse sideways is a bit more of an advanced skill, but is a useful one. You will use it to solve some of the twelve problems. Start by standing in the middle of your training area, facing your horse. You are going to make the horse move to your left at first, so hold the rope in your left hand and the stick in your right. With you standing still, use your rope to get him to back away from you. Get him to stand about 6 – 8 foot away from you and open your left arm away from your body to suggest that your horse moves that way, use your stick to encourage him to step sideways and to keep his body straight. Your biggest problem is likely to be him moving forwards towards you, so be ready to shake the rope to have him step backwards. After you have moved him to your left, swap over the rope to your right and the stick to your left, and try to move him sideways to the right. Most horses are initially better in one direction than the other, but work to balance them out.

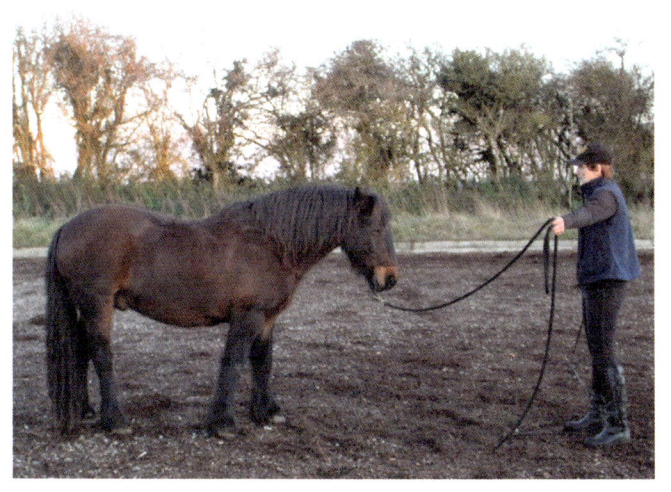

Moving sideways

Making a training plan

You've described your problem, and assembled your equipment. The last thing to do before you get started is make a training plan. Don't overwhelm yourself, start by planning your first week of training, and be prepared to adjust your plan as you go depending on results.

There isn't a 'one size fits all' plan. Your plan must be built on the idea of how horses learn and you'll have to consider many things when drawing one up:

- What are your horse's main worries?
- How intelligent is he?
- How good is his memory?
- What does he like to do?
- What does he not like?
- Which is his favourite side?
- What needs improving physically?
- What needs improving mentally?

Here's some examples. Say your horse takes his time slowing down and you want to improve this. Your best approach is to incorporate lots of transitions into your plans: trot – stop – back up – trot and so on. But maybe you've contributed to the problem? When you shorten your reins does your horse get excited? If so then you might need to build some psychology balance into your plan. When you shorten your reins, just keep walking, then release your reins and do a working trot to help change his mind about what shortening reins means (see the chapter about the horse with no brakes for some more ideas).

You must incorporate both physical balance and psychological balance into your plan. Success is measured by doing things equally well on both sides, in-hand or under saddle. So your horse should trot a 20 metre circle equally well on both reins, or he should move sideways equally well to the left or the right.

So your plan is built around what your horse needs, but you also need to be honest with yourself about how many days a week you will be able to train him for. You must also include working on yourself as part of your plan; you need to develop some new skills too. One of these is being observant. If you want to be a better leader for your horse, then you must be in control of the smallest thing. The more that your horse knows that you can read even the tiny changes, the more he will see you as a good leader.

When I was in primary school we had an amazing school manager who seemed to know everything about every pupil. If someone dropped their average score by only 1% she'd want to know what the problem was. When someone's score went up, she would congratulate them. We all used to assemble in the morning before class, and she could observe the 45 queues and instantly pick up if a boy was wearing trainers or a girl was wearing make-up. There was no way you could do anything wrong without her finding out.

You need to be like that school manager with your horse. You want to be able to read him and spot any changes for good or bad. So you need to be conscious of developing these skills when you're making your plan. Don't ever make him regret listening to you, or worry about a mistake that he's made, because that's when your relationship can go wrong. You don't want him to fear you or ignore you, and his life should be better if he trusts and respects you.

Your plan must be interactive. You write down what exercises you're going to do on what days, and then you make a note on your plan of how many repetitions you did, and how many were good and how many not so good. You can then note how many good days you've had in a row, and that will help you make your plan for the next week. While you're doing this, you'll be building on your knowledge of your horse. You'll be training yourself to observe how many repetitions you usually need, when you can ask for the next level, or whether you need to introduce some psychology balance before you ask for more.

You also need to be looking out for the 'signs' that show a horse has had a good learning experience. For example, a sign that you have succeeded with the in-hand sideways exercise is that your horse keeps straight as he moves sideways.

Here's an example plan that someone starting out at the very beginning of their training has made. They've set themselves the task of working through the exercises described in this chapter; to start their horse and get themselves familiar with the feeling they're looking for and with observing their horse.

Day	Activities	Notes
Mon	Something and Nothing	quite anxious about string at first - settled after 10 mins
Tues	Something and Nothing Backing up	good with S&N - backing needs work licking and chewing!
Weds	—	—
Thurs	Something and Nothing Backing up	3 good back ups!
Fri	—	—
Sat	Something and Nothing Backing up Moving front and back end	3 good back ups, OK with moving back end - front end finds difficult walking forward a bit
Sun	Something and Nothing Backing up Moving front and back end	3 good front ends and back ends each side

Chapter 5
Catching your Horse

Can you catch your horse? In the ideal world your horse waits patiently for you to catch him, or better still he'll come to 'catch' you. But if you're having problems, this could be due to a number of reasons. Maybe your horse is genuinely scared or worried? If the problem has occurred suddenly, something might have happened in the field overnight that has really upset him. Maybe your horse really isn't scared, but has a good idea that you want to work him hard or take him away from his friends and he is keen to avoid that.

The reluctant horse

When you have a horse that doesn't want to be caught because he knows that means he's going to be ridden, or at least taken away from the grass and his friends to be put in the stable, you have to work on two things. Firstly you have to work on the 'psychology balance'. You need to teach him that every time he is caught it does not mean work or isolation; give him lots of reasons to enjoy coming in. Secondly, you have to get your horse to understand that running away from you doesn't work.

Remember that 'psychology balance' is balancing the pleasant and the not-so-pleasant. How would you feel if every time a friend came to call, they wanted you to do something for them, or wanted to pull and poke you around to try out a new hairstyle? You might not always be so pleased to see them! They need to take you somewhere nice or just spend time with you with no pressure once in a while to restore the balance. Whether your horse is scared, or just fed up, you need to convince them that being with you, and being caught, might just be a good thing.

For example, say I go to the field one day to bring in my horse to ride, and for the first time ever he isn't keen to be caught. What I might do then is bring him in and give him something nice to eat, and put him straight back into the field. I will visit him later in the day, holding a halter or headcollar, but just stroke him without catching him and then walk away. If that goes well, I would maybe catch him and ride him the next day. But I would always try to find opportunities to just go and spend time with him without making demands. The idea is that my horse never knows why I'm visiting; I might be going to bring him in to feed him or fuss him rather than ride, or I might just want to say 'hi'.

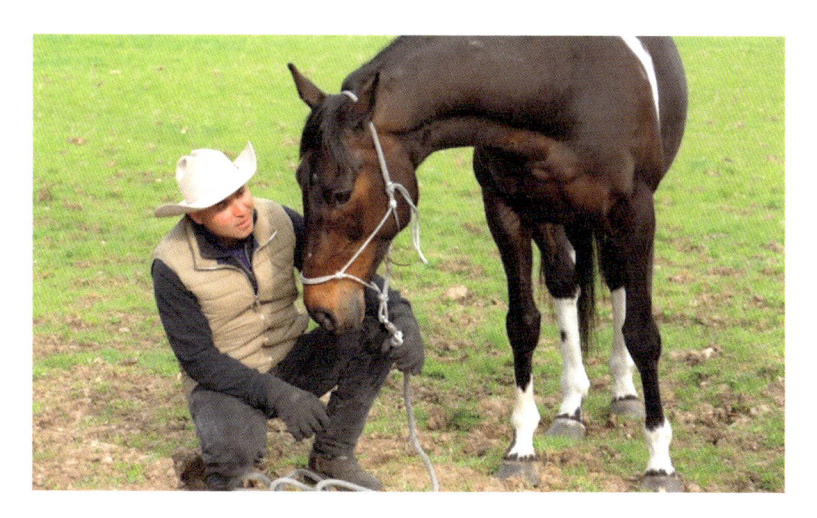

How do you cope if your horse keeps running away from you? You must convince him that running away does not work, but this takes time and patience. If you go to get your horse and he runs away, you must not leave the field until you at least have the horse standing still and facing you. This might take several hours, but you need to persist! (maybe you can use some temporary fencing to make the field smaller before you start). My longest catching problem took me a whole day from 7 am to 8 pm in the field, just to end up stroking the horse and leaving. The next day took from 7 am to 11 am for the first touch, I then left and came back that afternoon and it only took me one hour to get near the horse to stroke him. After seven days of this exercise the horse learned to not run away, he found out that it wasn't worth it.

The timid horse

If you have a horse that is genuinely scared of humans then you will need to build trust more gradually. Such a horse needs to see people every day who do not ask him to do anything, or even try to catch him. You shouldn't try to progress until this horse is happy with people passing near him and doesn't try to run away from them. You should have people just walking past the horse for three to seven days, and have at least three good experiences in succession on each day before you consider this phase to be complete. The next step is going to the horse's shoulder. Keep doing this until the horse stops and looks at you and waits. This is called a 'positive freeze', because he does it out of choice. After you can do this for seven times per day over seven days (the days don't have to be consecutive), you can progress to the 'freeze and touch'. Proceed as before, but this time hold out your hand for the horse to sniff; let him choose to touch your hand. After you have successfully repeated this seven times over seven days, you can try to touch and rub the horse's withers. Again repeat this for the 7/7 formula. Now you are ready to start catching your horse, but be wary if you need to expose him to a demanding situation like the vet or farrier, because you can easily lose his trust again. Every horse is likely to be different in this situation. Some will gain trust in you really quickly, while others take much longer. But all horses can learn not to run away.

The suddenly scared horse

A horse that becomes suddenly scared overnight is normally one that requires work on trust and confidence away from the field, ideally keep him stabled while you work on this. For this type of horse there are four important steps that you need to go through. First build his confidence by exposing him to lots of different things that he sees and hears while you have him on the halter and rope. The second step is to do some loose training, including 'follow me', and 'stand still if I am on my way to you'. The third step is to lead the horse from the side around his field. Lead him all around the field, from both sides, until you have at least three good experiences in a row with the horse feeling totally relaxed. When he is relaxed you can stop and let him graze at your side. At this point you should review his field mates: are they spooky, fearful horses? Maybe he would benefit from being turned out with some calmer friends? If this is not possible, increase the time you spend working with him from the ground, and walking him round the field. The fourth and final step is to start turning him out again. Begin with turning him out for limited hours during the day for the first week. When you, or anyone else, can go up to your horse in the field every hour and rub him, start leaving him for longer intervals between visiting. If he starts to be fearful again, shorten the intervals (horses can hang on to bad memories). When you can visit and rub your horse every four to five hours, you can start leaving him out overnight again.

How to get a horse to follow you

A horse looks for a leader to trust and to learn from, and also to go in front of him and check that the area is safe and protect him. Most horses expect their leader to be another horse, but we can teach them that we can be just like one of them and be safe to follow, and life becomes much easier for us!

Horses learn from pressure and release, and if we can learn to master this technique we can get them to do things for us and with us. Applying pressure means putting a horse out of his comfort zone by using voice signals or physical force using your stick, and you must keep this pressure up until the horse follows us, or, at the very beginning of training, faces us. Then you give him release by walking away. Repeat this after a few seconds or minutes. Aim to get more each time, maybe facing you and taking one step towards you, then next time facing you and taking a few steps towards you. Don't rush; always remember that you are working with the next day in mind. Stop at a nice point, so that your horse has a good reason to be pleased to see you the next day.

For example, if I want a horse to follow me, I like to first make sure that the horse is not scared of me, or anything that I'm carrying. Before I start with this, I should have done enough work with the horse to know that we can communicate and that I can control his go, slow, left and right. I will begin in a confined space with him (if you don't have access to a pen, try building yourself one in the field with posts and electric fence tape). When a horse is loose, and I want him to follow, all I need to do is apply pressure on him, he might go left or right, trying to get away, but I'll block his exit and put pressure on. As soon as he stops, turns and faces me, I release him. After he has learned to face me to get results, he will next try a step towards me. In the first days I will be looking for just a few steps and ending on a good note. I'll keep building up gradually and balancing things out (if you ask your horse too much, too soon, he might start to refuse to follow).

Chapter 6
Leading your Horse

Leading a horse can tell you a lot about the relationship that you have with him, and how much he views you as a leader. When I go to help someone with their horse, one of the first things that I like to see is them leading. I use this as a diagnostic tool.

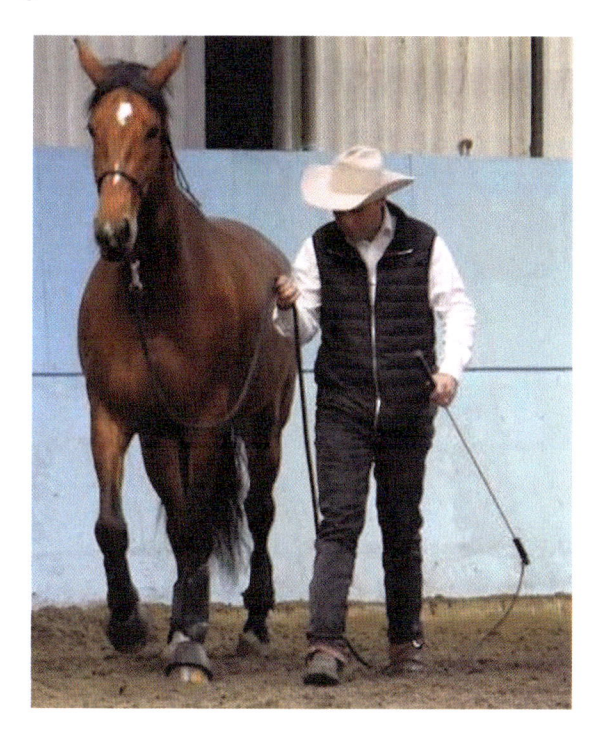

First of all I look for the positives in the relationship. If the horse being led is showing that he feels comfortable and safe with his owner, even if he's not listening very well, it means that he knows his handler won't hurt him. I want to build on that basic trust.

After finding the positives I start looking for the weaknesses in the relationship, and what is missing from the person's leadership skills. I look for who moves first and how, and for how aware the leader is of their body language.

Normally I will ask the person to lead the horse up and down a few times, watching how they stop and change direction. Do they ask for forward in the same way each time? Do they stop and turn in the same way? I also look at who is leading who. Does the horse follow the owner, or is it the other way around? I like to see the leader head for a certain destination to see what happens, and will often set up three cones in the arena. I then ask the leader to head from one cone to another. Most people can reach the destination cone, though far fewer can stand still next to it. Unfortunately, if you want to build a unique relationship with your horse, it's not about the destination so much as the journey. There are many ways to reach a goal with a horse, but they are not all as good as each other. Think about your own life, there are many ways to earn a living, but the best way is doing something that you love that helps other people at the same time. Not all of us are lucky enough to get a job like that, but at least you can make your relationship with your horse as valuable as it can be.

When I'm watching someone lead their horse from cone to cone, I normally find that when they ask their horse to go forward he turns into them, then they turn away, and the horse turns into them again. They can end up circling several times before they reach their destination. This tells me that the leader has no control of their horse's nose and feet. Remember that wherever the nose goes, the body follows.

One of the big problems that people have on the ground is that they are unaware of their body language, and of what they need to do to go forward and back, left and right. They especially have no control of their horse's nose. Many of these people are good riders and are in full control of their horse's nose when they are in the saddle. They could go straight from cone to cone very easily if they were riding rather than leading. When you are on board you have two reins to control the nose, you can move the head left or right and the body follows. When leading, you only have a rope, and can only use that to move the nose towards you. You need some substitute for the outside rein and that's where the stick comes in.

If you watch a mare communicate with her foal, you'll see that the mum will use her nose to push her foal away from her. For example, say the foal is standing next to her right shoulder, she will push his nose to the right to move him right. Then if she wants to move him forward she will swish her tail (just like we can use a string on the stick). If she wants to turn him closer to her, she turns her nose away, inviting him to come closer into that space, using her tail again to encourage him to move. When the mare wants to stop her foal, she stops first. If the foal doesn't stop she will use her mouth to tell him off for passing her shoulder.

As a leader we can use similar language as the mare to communicate with our horse. I personally like to lead horses from different zones:

- From the front
- From the side
- From behind

There are endless variations on these positions – slightly to one side, slightly more forward, slightly more backwards and so on. For the instructions in this chapter we are going to concentrate on leading from in front and leading from the side. What is important is that you know where you are going and how you are going to get there, and you are in full control of your horse's nose and feet. When leading from a particular zone, it must be you that makes any change. Do not let the horse change the zone for you. For example, if you start leading from in front, don't find that your horse has suddenly decided that you should be leading from his shoulder.

If a horse is to see you as a leader in every sense of the word, you must have as much control of where and when they move as a mare would have with her foal. The more you show them awareness of how you are using your own body, the more chance you have of taking this role in their eyes. In any relationship the 'release' is important. Just like a mare lets her foal run around and play, you must let your horse have a good time, and a free time, when you are around. Think of it like a relationship between human parents and their kids. When does the party start in your house, when you leave or when you come home? If your kids are happy and excited when you come home, then you are a good leader and your kids like to have you around. This doesn't mean that they don't respect you; but you should build that respect from trust, understanding, and making them feel safe and comfortable. Comfortable means that they are happy to be themselves but are also happy to observe their boundaries (boundaries that are built on the right type of respect).

Leading from the front

If, when you lead your horse from the front, you find that he hesitates or pulls back and freezes when you pull on the rope, then something is missing from your relationship. Maybe mistakes were made in the way he has been led or trained from the very beginning. Before you start working to correct this, make sure you fully understand the pressure and release rules (go back and read these again in Chapter 4 if you're not completely sure about them).

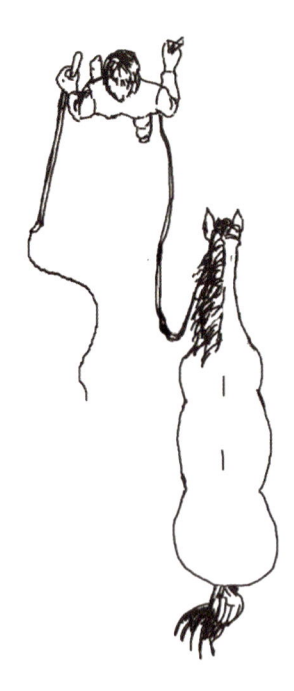

leading from the front

As a preparation, get a friend to act the horse role for you for a while. You hold the rope and they hold the halter. Think about what the first thing you do is when you pull the horse towards you. You shouldn't go straight to a pressure that you cannot maintain. The moment that you begin pulling you are not going to stop until the 'horse' puts a foot forward, but remember to release the pressure the instant that he does. A 'greedy' leader who never releases the pressure is someone that a horse finds hard to trust and rely on.

When you've practiced with your friend, and are happy with your pressure, and your release reactions, then you can try it with your horse. Pull the rope and if your horse responds by stepping forward, instantly release. Even if he stops straight away, give him a minimum of five seconds to think before you put the pressure back on. Use this technique to teach him to become lighter in his response to pressure behind his ears. Pressure here should always mean 'forwards'. When you lead a horse from the front you should aim to be able to do quick and soft transitions between stop, walk and trot, and back to stop again.

You can swish with your stick and string to help get your horse moving but if you have a very lazy and stubborn horse, and believe that no amount of pulling and swishing will get him moving, then you can enlist the help of a friend. Your friend is going to act as your 'D' pressure, to be used when your horse will not listen to A, B or C, and your ultimate aim is to be able to do it without them. It is important that you and your friend have a clear plan of what to do, and practice it away from the horse. Get your friend to do some 'something and nothing' exercises using the stick with your horse to ensure that your horse isn't going to be frightened. If that goes well, get your friend to stand a safe distance behind your horse, and begin adding pressure when you ask (it's important that they don't start until you ask). Then they should begin gently and rhythmically tapping his hindquarters with the string. They need to keep up the same rhythm until the horse moves, and then instantly release. At the same time, you must release the pressure on the rope. Release for a minimum of five seconds, then, if he has stopped, start applying pressure again. Always start again with an 'A' pressure, you must give your horse a chance to change for the better and react to a small pressure. If you don't do this, how can you expect change to happen? Make sure that you work enough on this exercise to ensure that you can lead him from the front on your own, without the help of your friend.

Leading from the side

The most important skill that you need in order to lead from the side is full control of your horse's nose. Start by teaching him the 'move the front end' exercise really well, so that he is used to moving his nose away when you ask with the stick. The stick is going to act as your 'outside rein' when you are leading from the side. You should also have taught your horse to back up before you begin leading from the side.

leading from the side

When you think you are ready, put yourself next to your horse's shoulder with the rope in your inside hand and the stick in your outside hand. When you're ready, ask the horse to move forward. A slight change in body language – leaning slightly forward – might be enough to get him moving, but otherwise swish the string in rhythm behind you, like a mare would use her tail. If the horse moves forward go with him, otherwise add more pressure with your string. If he hasn't moved after three seconds add some physical pressure by touching his back end with the string. As soon as he moves you must instantly remove the pressure and move with the horse.

When you have mastered walking, begin practicing transitions. Walk forwards, stop, and then back up. You can add in a snaking exercise where you deliberately move left and right and get your horse to follow your route. Start getting your horse to turn towards you and away from you. Don't wait until you need this control, build the language and communication before you need it.

Signs of a good leader

The signs of a good leader are firstly that the horse feels safe and comfortable next to you. Secondly the horse will move forwards and backwards, and left and right when you ask him to. Your horse should begin to lose the 'OMG!' reaction when you correct him, or when he's done something wrong. He can do all this without any fear.

The best sign is that, when your horse feels concerned about something, he asks you if it is alright to keep moving. To me, nothing is more rewarding than that moment of trust. I can't describe the feeling I get whenever my horse is unsure about something, and all I need to do is tell him 'don't worry, continue' with my body language.

Chapter 7
Grooming your horse

In this chapter I'm going to help you with any problems that you might have when brushing your horse, but also with any difficulties you experience picking out his feet, and getting him shod.

Before I start talking about grooming your horse I'd like to say a word or two about how you tie your horse up. The length of the rope that you give him is important for the safety of both of you. Put simply, the longer the rope, the more potential danger there is. Years ago I used to tie with a long rope, thinking that it was kinder, but with more experience I realised just how much damage a horse can do to himself when he gets tangled in his rope and panics. As well as the length of the rope, you must also be conscious of the length of the string that you tie him to. Together the length of the rope and string should mean that your horse cannot physically reach lower than his knee. If you tie up your horse to eat from a bucket on the ground, then stay with him until he's finished. You might get away with using a long rope for years, but then it can all suddenly go wrong, and severe injuries might result.

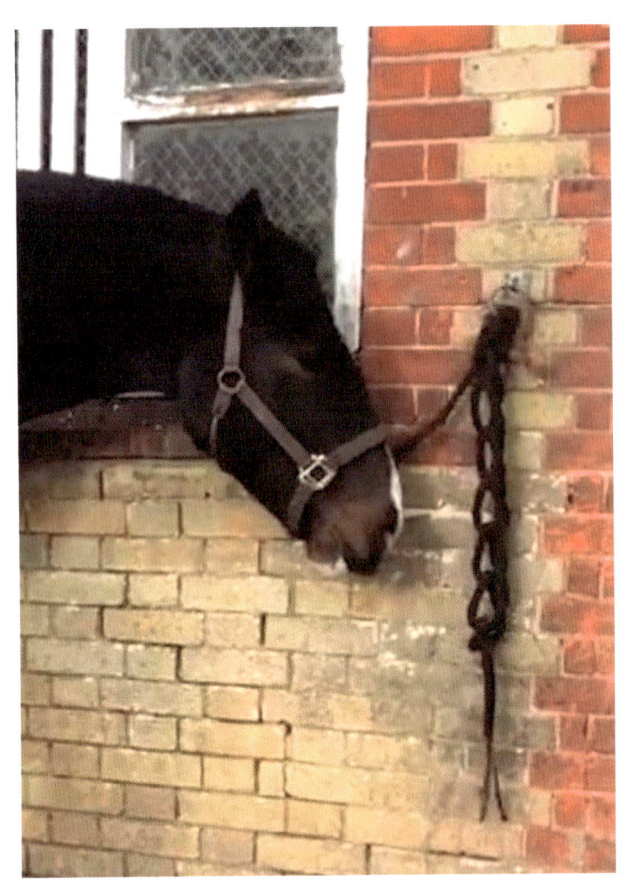

correct way to tie up

With your horse tied up safely, it's time to get started. You need to ensure that you have the minimum of language and tools to communicate when something goes wrong.

When I work with people who have problems with grooming, or with picking up feet, I find that 90% of the time the issues are due to insufficient preparation: the basics are just not there. When a horse is tied up, he should not give us trouble, but if we never teach a horse to respect us, he learns to ignore us instead. This horse expects you to move out the way when he moves his back end or front end, and he will often move his back end towards you to try and stop you doing something he doesn't like. Such a horse isn't doing this to hurt you, you have inadvertently taught him to ignore you and come into your space. Horses do this to each other, it's natural. Most of the time they are not trying to be dominant, but something happens that they don't like, or they lose patience, and so they move out of the way.

How can you improve situations like this? In preparation, you should have done the 'something and nothing' exercise and the 'moving the back end away' exercise described in Chapter 4. Do them somewhere like your arena to begin with. You should then bring the stick to him while he's tied up and run it all over him. Your aim is to be able to rub him everywhere from his nose to his tail and from his back to his feet. If your horse is a bit unsure of the stick in this situation, don't start by touching his nose or he might pull back. Concentrate on touching him behind the withers, on his back or hindquarters. Anywhere in front of the withers might be interpreted as a 'go backwards' command. If your horse moves, do your best to keep the stick on and keep rubbing (while keeping yourself safe) until he stops. When he does stop, take the stick off for four or five seconds, and then start rubbing again.

If you are happy that you've had three good times of rubbing your horse all over both sides, then you can start teaching him to move side to side at your command. Stand on his left and, with a nice rhythm, use the stick to ask your horse to move his back end away from you. Remember to start with as soft a pressure as possible and don't increase it too much, even if he does the opposite and moves into your pressure (because he's been doing that for years and getting comfort). All you need to do is keep tapping in the same pressure, the same rhythm, without anger until he moves his back end away, and then rub him with the stick to reward him. Always remember to wait until you are completely ready before you start. Once you have started, you can't stop until you get a result, otherwise you will need a stronger pressure or a longer time to get a result the next time that you try. When you have succeeded with one side, move to the other side and repeat.

The point of moving hindquarters from one side to the other is firstly to have more communication and build more leadership and respect. The aim is to be able to say things to your horse like 'move a little bit this way' or 'stay that distance away'. The other reason is so that the horse has a much better idea of where his boundaries are. He must learn to respect the human being standing next to him, and not move his back end into their space to shift them away. He must realise that if there's a person on his left, for example, that that side is 'closed' to him, and he must not step into it. He can go forwards or backwards or to the right or he can stand still. The horse is seeking comfort and he will find that this comes when he is standing still. So he learns to seek his comfort in a much more positive way, rather than just by squeezing or pushing his handler away. Horses are clever. In the moment that they know you are not going to hurt them, but that you're not going to give up, they will find that the shortest way is to stand still and be calm.

If you are able to do these first two exercises really well, moving your horse backwards or sideways with an A pressure, and you feel that your horse has responded well and no longer moves into you, then you can start on the next exercise of rubbing and grooming.

Grooming

When I'm going through this process, I normally like to start with my hands. I'm checking for areas that the horse is particularly sensitive about (I might already have a good idea about these from the stick-rubbing exercise). So start rubbing your horse with your hands. If you have a difficult horse and he's only just starting to respect you when he's tied up, you should keep your stick nearby while you are rubbing, so that you can reach it and use it if the horse starts moving into you again. He might do this if you start doing something that he doesn't like, so be ready to tap and move his back end away again. I suggest that you try to keep an eye on his ears. When you rub any area that he finds unpleasant, you will see him respond with his ears, you need to rub this area more until he puts his ears back to 'neutral'.

When you are doing this exercise, watch out for any pain issues on their back or stomach, or any other areas. I have found that many horses are sensitive in some areas, but with only a few of them is this due to pain. A simple way of checking is to repeat rubbing the area that they have reacted to. If the reaction lessens as you repeat, this is a sign that it is not associated with pain. If your horse is experiencing pain then the reaction will get worse, not better.

When you are confident about rubbing your horse, you can decide that it's time to start rubbing with a brush. As with rubbing with your hands, the release is everything here. Some horses can be in a very bad place about brushing, they can bite, rear and kick to try and avoid it. So long as they are tied up safely, you should persist until they stop, then you must stop too. After a few seconds, repeat the exercise. Increase the time that you are brushing slowly. You are trying to give him a reason for being brushed, and even a grumpy and sensitive horse can learn this.

If your horse has reacted to being brushed in the past by trying to kick you, then keep your stick to hand, and move his back end away from you if he tries that. Be ready for any amount of repetition to deal with this, and never get angry. It is important that you don't release the pressure; you might have to stop brushing for safety's sake, but so long as you are tapping, you haven't released.

When he has learned the 'if you stop, I stop' lesson well, you could start introducing the occasional food treat as a reward. But don't do this with a 'bitey' horse, and don't use food as a bribe, at most it's an irregular pleasant surprise for him. The right time to introduce food rewards is when you can brush him everywhere on both sides three days in a row without him reacting. When you observe that your horse is standing there quietly, with his ears in 'neutral', that is the time to reward him. Give him a food reward during some sessions, and in some sessions, don't.

You can also use psychology balance to get your horse to start viewing being brushed as a reward. With your horse tied up, you can keep moving his back end. Move it three times to the right, then three times to the left, then brush him when you stop. Keep repeating this sequence, and when he is relaxed with the brushing, maybe end the session with a food reward. The horse will start looking forward to being released and brushed. You can even do this exercise in the school. For example, move his hind end for five steps, then stop and brush. Keep repeating moving for 5 steps followed by brushing for about 10 -20 seconds. You stopping to brush will become his favourite time.

There are many, many ways we can give our horses reasons to do things for us, but you should aim to do at least the minimum for him. But I hope you will do more than the minimum for your most beloved animal and partner in life!

Lifting the feet

With the legs, one of the important things that you have to teach the horse is that he keeps his foot on the ground while you rub the leg. Many people see it as desirable that a horse picks the foot up as soon as you move towards it. But say that you want to feel the digital pulse or check the tendons? It is much better that you train him to lift his feet to a more specific command. Also some horses pick their feet up in a fearful way, because they want to avoid you touching their legs. Your being able to touch your horse's legs without him moving them is a sign that he is confident. A horse learns from everything he sees, hears or feels, and categorises them all as a 'something' or a 'nothing'. You want your horse to regard anything touching his legs as a 'nothing' until you explicitly ask him to lift his feet.

After you have got to the stage where you can rub all four legs without the horse moving into you, you can begin to work on picking his feet up. As you prepare to do this, have the pressure and release rules at the forefront of your mind. I like to use a bit of squeezing pressure from tendons down to fetlock to ask the horse to lift a foot. Don't change the pressure and don't use a pressure that you can't maintain. A constant squeeze is my A and B pressure, but I always have another plan in mind if the horse does not comply. I might start squeezing in the chestnut area, or, if I know the horse is OK with it, I might start tapping on the leg (for example, with a hoofpick). This is the C pressure. However much pressure you use, you must release it the instant that the horse lifts his foot for you. All you need at first is two quiet seconds holding his foot up, then you can put it down.

Be safe, wear gloves and maybe a riding hat before you start picking up feet. With the back feet, initially just lift the foot towards the tummy. Don't pull it backwards so that you can see his sole.

Some horses have been inadvertently taught to ignore pressure. Some horses use ignoring the pressure as a technique to tire their handler. It is very easy for a horse to learn this lesson. For example, if you started squeezing his leg to ask him for a pick up, but stopped squeezing – even for two or three seconds - before he'd done it, this is all the horse needs to learn the 'ignoring' lesson. Next time you will need a longer duration or a higher pressure before the horse complies.

Release is the moment of understanding for a horse, and you must be the one who releases the pressure at the right time. It could take two, three, or even five minutes of pressure to reach this stage, but some horses will pick up within 20 seconds. If you are dealing with a horse that has previously been difficult, it is more likely to take a long time than a short time. Mentally, you have to be ready to face some difficulties and deal with them in the right way.

If you reach the point where you can pick up all four feet for two seconds, and you have done this three good times in a row, then you can start increasing the time that you hold the foot up for. You don't have to do all this on the same day, you can spread it over a few days. Remember to rub the leg both before and after each lift. The rubbing is the reward.

You need to reach the point where you are able to pick up each foot for about 20 seconds before you begin picking them out with a hoofpick, or changing the position of the back leg. Spread this over at least a week, the more you rush the longer it might take you!

Pick out each foot gently and slowly, start by just picking out a bit, don't aim to clear out the whole foot at first. The more steps you break it down into, the better.

Preparing for the farrier

If your horse has had an issue with farriers all his life, don't run the risk of ruining all the good work you've just done by assuming that he'll be fine from now on. The farrier is not you, and the positions that he uses and the length of time that he must hold the horse's foot up for are different. Your horse might also be alarmed by the sounds and the smells of a farrier's visit. You have to prepare your horse for all of this too.

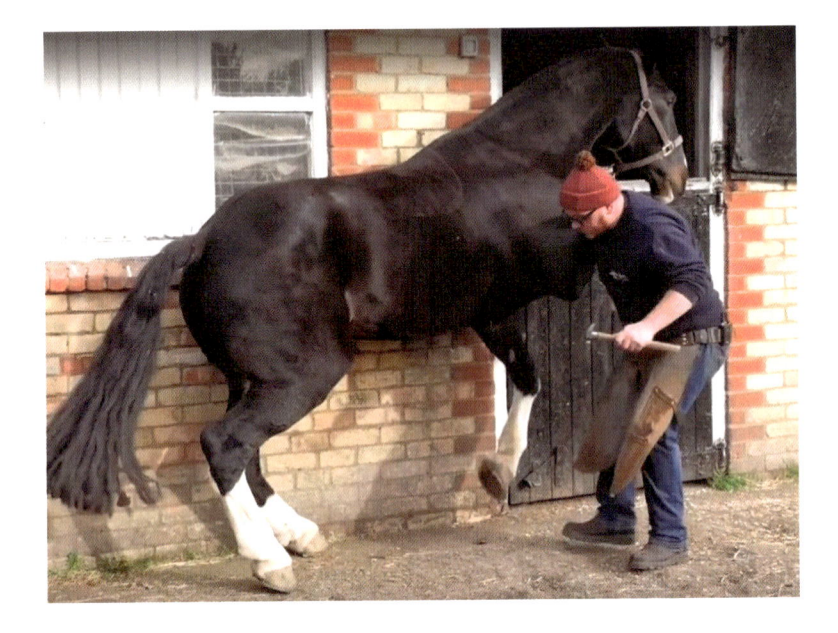

How do you prepare him? After you've done all the steps for picking out his feet, you need to start increasing the time that each foot is held up for. Your aim is to hold each foot up for five minutes for a minimum of three good days in a row. Then start impersonating a farrier and holding your horse's leg like he or she would. When your horse is happy with that, bring a small hammer and an old shoe and start rhythmically banging on the shoe next to the horse. When he's calm about that, start doing it next to his feet (keep yourself safe and be ready to move). When he's happy with you doing that next to all four feet, get a friend to help you by banging the shoe while you hold the foot up. If he's good about all four feet for a minimum of three times each, then you can start banging on the foot itself. Hit the foot gently and rhythmically.

Another preparation is to get some hoof offcuts from somewhere and burn them next to the horse on both sides (you could buy a cheap, portable barbecue to burn them in). This helps get the horse used to the smell and the smoke. Again, aim for a minimum of three good days.

Ideally the next stage is to get your farrier to come and pay your horse a visit, but without actually intending to shoe him. Get your farrier to rub your horse's legs and pick up his feet just like you did. See if he or she can hold all the legs in the required positions, rubbing afterwards each time as a reward. If this goes OK then you can book the farrier to come and actually shoe him, but you must keep up your good work until the appointed day.

Make sure that you exercise your horse just before he is shod. Ride him or lunge him so that he doesn't have extra energy. Set up for the shoeing in a place where your horse feels comfortable, then do at least fifteen minutes of preparation before the farrier starts working on him. If you have successfully done all the preparation, and not rushed anything, there is no reason why your horse should not now be good to be trimmed and shod.

Chapter 8
The Spooky Horse

Remember that the horse is a prey animal. From the moment that they are born they know that they must run from anything they hear, see or feel that they are unsure about. This makes sense when you consider that their survival might depend on reacting this way. They act like it's the end of the world because it might be the end of their world.

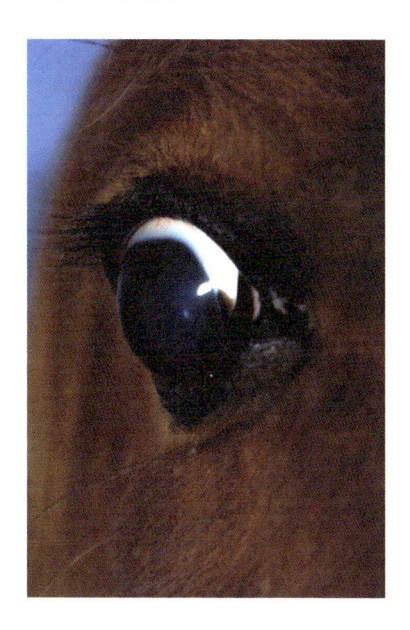

To be able to ride horses, or even just to handle them, we have to teach them to behave in exactly the opposite way. If the horse encounters something he's not sure about, he must stand still and not worry, but wait for instructions from you. It might take time to get there with a horse, but with the right knowledge and with practice you can do it.

There are three basic types of spookiness:

1. **Spooked by a sound**. This could be the sound of something that they can't actually see, but is something that they have a bad memory of. Maybe something happened the last time they heard it and they had to run. It might have been something that they remember other horses, or even their mother, running away from. They can also be scared by a new sound. What will happen if that sounds stops while they are still scared of it? They will add it as a bad memory and it becomes a 'something' rather than a 'nothing'.

2. **Spooked by a sight**. Horses have a fantastic picture memory of places that they are familiar with. They know every detail of their field, their stable, the arena where you ride them, and their regular hacking routes. This memory is even more detailed in a horse that lacks confidence, and extends to things like the colour of the ground. Such a horse sees it as an essential survival skill to notice when anything changes. They might be scared of something like a different water bucket in the corner of their stable. This horse is likely to spook when something has appeared in (or even

disappeared from) his environment. Horses can be spooked by the sight of something new that is approaching from the front or behind, or that they have to go past. If a horse sees something that he was scared of the last time he encountered it, and you have not taught him not to fear it, then he will be scared of it the next time he sees it.

3. **Spooked by feel**. Horses can be spooked by something that touches them as they are ridden or lead. This could be something like leaves, grass, stones – anything that you pass that touches their body, legs or feet – they can retain this memory of a different material touching them.

You need to teach your horse to be more confident, to not be scared any more, or at least to make their fear reactions much smaller and more manageable. How can you do this? There are many ways to help horses develop and increase their confidence, and these take lots of repetition and practice. But before you start, you need to take a few points on board:

- If your horse doesn't see you as his leader, building his confidence will be difficult. Why is this? Horses constantly feel the need to protect themselves, as a prey animal they know the best way to do this is by keeping their eyes and ears open for signs of anything that might threaten them. Their natural reaction is to run away. This is an instinct every horse is born with, and it is reinforced by what their mother has taught them to do. Even if their mother was herself confident and well trained, a horse still has the instinct to protect himself. If a foal sees that his mother is not scared in a particular situation, he will begin to classify this as 'nothing'. This foal then needs humans to teach him that they are not scary, and to touch him and ask him to do things, and in that way we are already changing our horses.

- If you want to take on the role of your horse's leader, you must know the basics really well. This starts with understanding how horses think, what they look for, and how they classify everything that they see, hear or feel as being 'something' or 'nothing'. You must also understand how every one of your movements is really important; you must get a result when you apply a pressure to horse, otherwise this will become 'nothing' in his mind. To be a leader, you must get your horse to both respect and trust you. The horse will listen to you when he regards you as the leader that cares about him and can protect him. When you are around, he doesn't need to worry anymore.

- Safety is what a horse seeks above everything. They can run miles in order to get to a place where they feel safe and that their life is not in danger. After safety they look for comfort and then food. If that is all in place, then they seek rest, play (and sex!).

There are four main things that you need to build on to increase your horse's confidence and to stop him being spooky:

1. Build your leadership. Teach your horse to trust and respect you and to listen to you. You must have the

language and communications skills to tell your horse when and how to move, and have full control of go, slow, left and right.

2. Reduce the role of instinct in your horse's behaviour. You must make the effects of his herd instinct, food instinct, home instinct, fight or flight instinct, or (for a mare or stallion) sex instinct much smaller. Be particularly aware of the effect of the herd instinct, as this can give you the most difficulties. So many times a horse can be scared without a horse companion. You will need to practice taking a horse away from his friends as often as it takes to make him confident to be with just you.

3. Desensitise your horse to his particular fears. Do this by exposing him to the feared thing, but stopping when the horse stands still and relaxes. Use the 7/7/7 formula to help you gauge your progress.

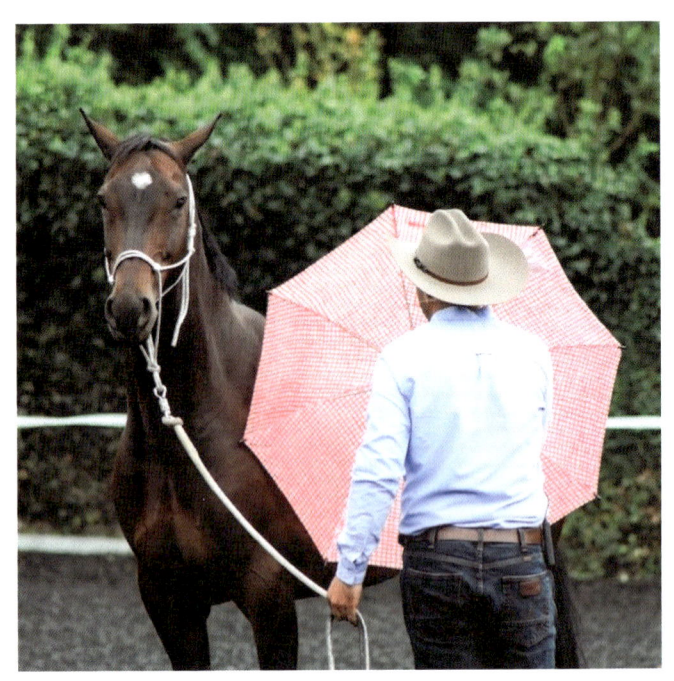

desensitising

4. Anticipate future problems. Try to recreate the things that bother your horse but in a safer environment. For example, if you are taking a horse to his first show, enlist the help of some friends to hold a 'mini-show' at home. Also think about whether your horse will cope with being away from his friends, how he will react when he encounters new horses. There is no end to the ways that you can make things easier for your horses.

Here are some examples of how you might deal with a spooky horse:

Say your horse is frightened by something he can hear but not see, for example rustling in the hedgerow – what predator might be lurking there? You don't need to actually ride by some rustling undergrowth to desensitise the horse to this. Build your leadership skills away from rustling bushes, then be creative in reproducing scary scenarios. Rustle some plastic bags to make a similar noise, and repeat this until you have three good days in a row. Then progress to some actual bushes. Do you know anyone with one or two well-trained dogs? Let the horse see them go in and out of the bushes and rustle all they like. The horse learns to recognise that these noises are being caused by the dogs and are nothing to do with him. When your horse is really good about this for three days in a row, try leading the horse past the bushes and getting a friend to jump out and surprise you. Repeat this for the 7/7/7 formula and you will know that you have done your job. (Remember, if you have real doubts that you will be able to complete one of these levels, then it is better not to start it.)

Say you have a horse with a very strong picture memory, you ride him in the same school that you ride in every day, but someone has moved the pooper-scooper to a different location – major drama! 'What is that doing there?' you can feel your horse thinking, 'OMG something is trying to kill me'. This horse needs a lot to change in his life on a very regular basis so that he can come to accept these changes. Start with working on the ground, and keep altering things in his environment. Change things in his stable, in his field, and everywhere you lead him. In the school, move things from the right to the left. Keeping passing and re-passing objects that your horse is unsure of until you feel him relax. Be patient, this can take a lot of time to work on. Some horses need a month or two of work like this, I have even known some that have taken up to a year. But all horses can get over this problem, as long as you don't give up. When a horse with a strong picture memory is brought up on a quiet yard where very little ever changes, then he can find it hard to accept change. It is much easier to go forward by exposing him to lots of stimuli so that he can learn to accept changes rather than trying to control every aspect of his environment.

In dealing with a spooky horse, we definitely can't control the wind or the rain and the sun, or other animals, but we can do our best to prepare our horse for a life that is full of surprises. Inevitably things will happen that scare our horse, but if we have prepared ourselves and him for this, then his fearful reactions will be smaller, and his trust in us will be bigger.

Chapter 9
Tacking up your Horse

It is quite likely that horses that have problems being tacked up also have problems being groomed. If you have already worked through the chapter on grooming, then you are in a good place to start working on problems with saddling and bridling. If not, I suggest you go back and read that chapter now, and do the basic 'something and nothing' and 'moving the back end' exercises, while the horse is tied up, before you proceed. This will give you the language to communicate with him before you start with the saddle or bridle.

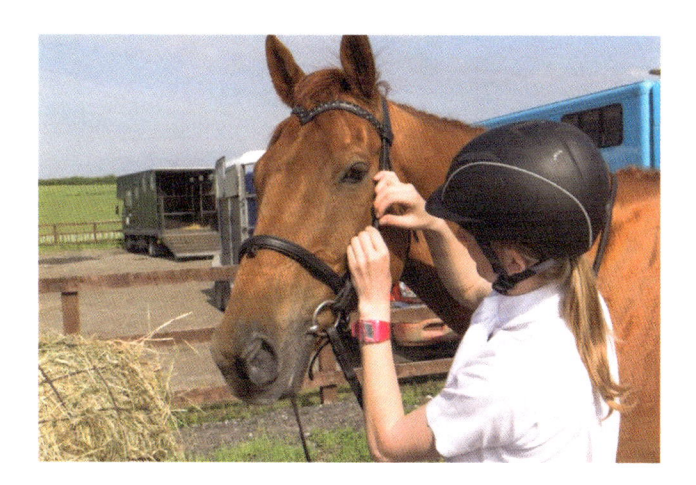

Before you start, please be aware that this chapter is aimed at horses who are used to having saddles and bridles on, but have a problem with it. It is not intended to help with young horses that have never had a saddle on before.

Saddling up

Start by letting your horse sniff the numnah or saddle pad. Let him sniff it from both sides and repeat until you get to the point where you can approach your horse with it and he ignores it. Then start rubbing him all over with the numnah. When he is relaxed about that, you can move on to working with the saddle.

Start by letting him sniff the saddle when it is on either side of him. When he is OK with that, put it on his back, slide it along and take it off again from the back end. Repeat this as many times as possible.

Many horses don't object to the saddle so much as the girth, but you can help a girth-shy horse and improve his reaction to it. Start with a rope. Take it around his back and belly. Hold the end coming down from the back with one hand. Use the other hand to hold the end coming under the belly as you would hold a girth. You then use the rope as a pretend girth to get him accustomed to the feeling of something tightening around him.

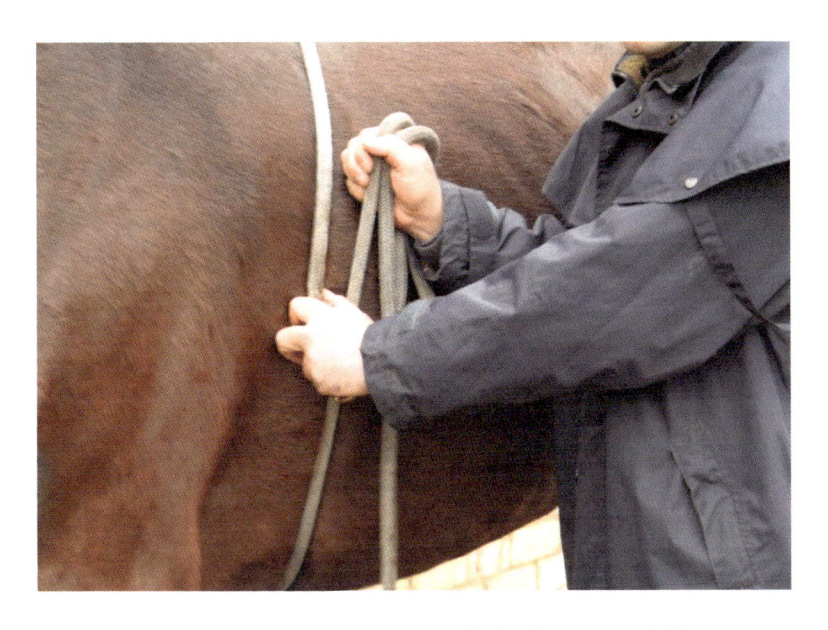

If you start pulling the rope up and the horse isn't happy, you have to keep the pressure up until the horse relaxes. Then release it for a few seconds before repeating. Normally the horse's problem is with the feeling of the girth being pulled up and fastened. You need to keep repeating the thing that the horse doesn't like: it's no good putting a saddle on and leaving him with the girth done up, that won't help. You have to keep repeating the tightening movement until he improves, or stops reacting altogether.

As with other areas of training, you are trying to give the horse a reason to be saddled up. Psychology balance is what is often missing. You can start introducing some psychology balance by exercising the horse in the arena (lunging or working with halter and stick), then take him to the tie up area. Put the saddle on, girth it up, then take it off. Repeat this until you have three good times in a row, and then end your session. Repeat for three days or more. This way, the horse comes to view the saddling up as the moment he gets release and comfort. You can even add food rewards to these moments. For example, after you've put the saddle on and off for a minimum of three times, you can give him a treat. This gives him more reasons to be saddled up. If you reach three good days in a row where you saddle and girth up, then the next day do the tacking up before you do the exercise in the arena. Some days ride your horse after you've tacked him up, and some days don't.

Bridling

Putting the bridle on is something that can go very wrong, and some horses really hate it, and can find a way to evade it quite easily. Big and strong horses find it especially easy to evade the bridle. There are many different issues connected to having the bridle on, and, as with others problems described in this book, you should start searching for the reasons behind your horse's objections:

- Is he scared?
- Is he sensitive?
- Is he in pain?
- Is he dominant?

When you have some idea of why, think about when he does it:

- Is it when you approach with the bridle in your hand?
- Is it the moment you take your hand up towards his ears?

- Is it when you try to get the bit in his mouth?

You have to isolate which bit of your body language 'sets him off'.

Your horse might be very sensitive behind his ears, or he might be reluctant to open his mouth for a human because experience tells him that it's always unpleasant when he does: it might be the bit, the wormer syringe, or the dentist (although if your horse does have mouth issues you should get his teeth checked). Every time your horse tries to explain he doesn't like it, he finds himself in trouble (that doesn't mean that his humans don't love him, just that they're exasperated).

Many people might have run out of tools by this point, and resort to hitting or shouting, trying to bribe them with treats, or singing or talking to sooth them. These tactics probably won't help, so you need to find a better way to communicate with your horse, and you won't find this if you don't look.

After you have worked out the why and the when of your bridling problem, you can start preparing your horse to accept his bridle without any drama.

I normally like to teach the horse the first two exercises really well: something and nothing and backing up. As part of the something and nothing, I rub the horse's ears until he stands still. If the ears are the cause of his issues, it can take a while to teach him that nothing can actually hurt him when the hands or the stick are above his ears. You can use your hands to rub, but if your horse is likely to rear, you should use your stick. The technique then is to keep rubbing with the stick until he comes down, when you release by removing the stick, and then rub again.

When you are able to rub the horse all over, behind his ears and on his face, and he is happy with it, you can begin lowering his head. Lowering the head is a proof of trust, and a horse that doesn't trust you will never lower his head at your command. Put one hand on the top of his head, just behind his ears, and the other on his nose, then put some pressure on to bring his head down. The horse is a prey animal, and needs to keep his head up to spot danger, so lowering his head for you is a way of him saying 'I trust you not to hurt me'.

When you start asking your horse to lower his head, you have to be ready to keep both hands on. If he raises his head and shakes one or both hands off, then you must be prepared to put them back straight away. Keep him uncomfortable until he complies, but don't panic or get angry with him. If the horse feels you losing your temper your task will become impossible. It must be like you're saying to him 'it's fine to move up or down, but I need to put my hands back'. Keep your hands on until your horse stands still for five seconds. If you have had a bit of a fight to reach this stage, then just standing still is enough for your horse to earn the reward of you moving your hands away for a good ten seconds. You are aiming to build on any positive behaviour.

When you put your hands back, you should now aim to get your horse to lower his head a bit more each time. The ultimate goal is to have him lower his head to the line of his chest. If you have control of moving his head up and down and left and right, you can bring the bridle, but take the bit off for the early stages (particularly if your horse is sensitive about the ears).

Start by rubbing him with the bridle before you try to put it on. Just keep rubbing him on both sides until he is happy with the sensation. Then lower his head and rub all over his ears with both hands while you are holding the bridle. Now put the bridle on and off as often as you need to. When you reach three good times in a row over three good days, you can start using your finger to open his mouth. If your horse's problems are with the bit, then work on this issue without the bit at first. Just open his mouth from the side using your fingers until he will hold it open for two seconds. You should reach the point when you can open his mouth while he's calmly licking and chewing.

When you've completed the steps above, the next thing is to work on getting your horse comfortable while you adopt the bridling position. It's important to do enough preparation. Sometimes we work on the ears and on opening the mouth, but neglect to work on body language and position. Sometimes we can be so focussed on getting the bridle on that we forget some of the subtleties. But the more you prepare, the simpler and easier it will be. Do everything like you're going to put the bridle on but without the actual bridle.

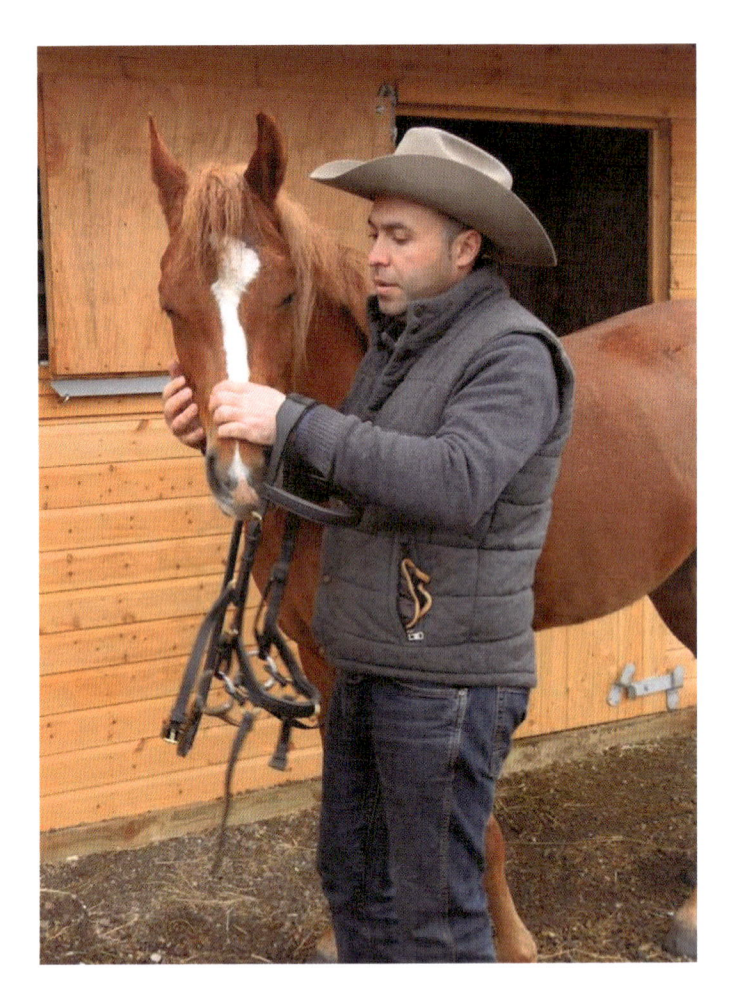

When you've worked on your position, bring the bridle to the horse. At first just stand in the bridling position, and put the bit under his chin. Then move the bit and put the headpiece over his ears. If he is good with both those moves, try putting the bit in his mouth, but don't put the headpiece over his ears yet. When he is happy with both of these, you can try actually putting the bridle on.

Like anything else, you can employ psychology balance in his training. For example, you can exercise him on the ground with the halter, and then put the bridle on and take him for a graze in hand while wearing it. There is no end to the variations you can try.

Chapter 10
The horse you can't get on

It can be very annoying if you have a horse that is a complete saint to ride, but an absolute devil to get on. The cause might be that he's genuinely nervous and tense about being mounted, or maybe he's worked out that being difficult is a way of avoiding work!

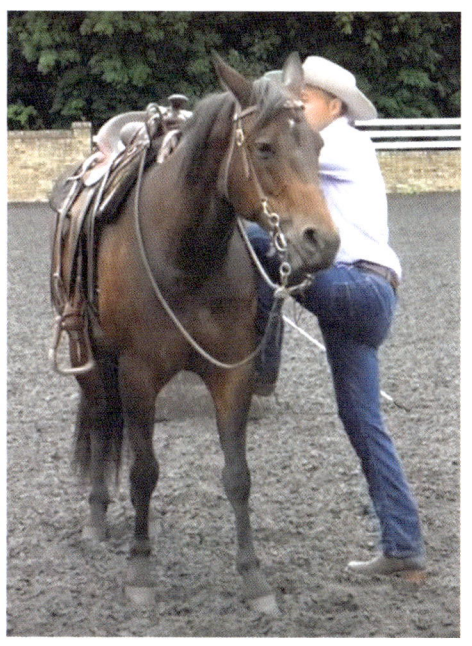

Sandy being a saint to get on

Most of the problems that show up in our horses have their roots in mistakes that we have previously made. It maybe that you've failed to notice the beginning of a mounting issue and have unwittingly let is escalate. Remember that most problems start small: you need to develop the skill to spot them, and to deal with them before they grow large and start interfering with your relationship with your horse.

If you usually use a mounting block, perhaps you didn't notice that the horse finds the area where the block is, or maybe the block itself, rather scary. He's got tense there, and been difficult when you got on, moving or spinning at just the wrong moment. This in turn has made you nervous, and that just acts as confirmation that he was right to be scared in the first place. It could equally be that your horse is a lazy (and smart) character. He fidgeted one day while you tried to mount, and you gave up rather than persisting. He's just found a great way to avoid work!

In the case of the nervous horse, you need to use psychology balance with him. You've got to give him reasons to change his feelings about the mounting block, and help him feel happy to come near it. If he is scared of being mounted from the ground, give him reasons to feel relaxed about that too.

In the case of the lazy horse, you have to work on your leadership skills. You need to be able to say to your horse 'you just stand still in this spot until I say different'. If you don't develop these skills, you will always find that you have issues in all sorts of areas.

In fact, both cases will benefit from both approaches. You must work on building your horse's confidence and trust, and his respect for your leadership. You must be able to say 'stand still on this particular spot', when that spot could be anywhere – next to the mounting block, the middle of a field, next to a trailer.

Sometimes a horse can be made to stand still by the fear of otherwise being in trouble. You can teach horses through this kind of fear, but it is not an approach that I can recommend. You do have to let a horse know that he has done wrong in a way that he can understand, but if he is not feeling 100% confident in you as leader, or 100% safe in his situation, then there is still a big chance that he will take off, spook or spin when you go to get on him. It is potentially so dangerous to get on a horse that won't stand still that this skill must be one of the most important foundations of your training. It is a 'home' area. Standing still next to you should be a place where the horse feels that nothing bad can happen to him.

Before you start on this training, I want you to be aware of two skills that you should be working to develop in yourself:

- Be more observant of your horse's thoughts and feelings so that you can spot when some anxiety develops. If fear does show up in your horse, be ready to put some time and effort into getting rid of it (before it gets rid of you). Your horse's concerns deserve some attention, a quick fix for today won't help tomorrow, and might actually make the problem worse.

- Be aware of how much control you have of your horse when you are on the ground. Can you control his feet? Can you get him to stand still in any location that you choose? Many horseriders are very good at controlling their horse from the saddle, but lack the same skills on the ground. You need to be able to control his nose, his tail, and his feet.

Stop riding your horse!

When you start working on your mounting problem, I would like you to take at least a week off from riding your horse. For the first three days, use just your halter, rope and stick, and don't even saddle him. Start with the something and nothing exercise to make sure that he is happy with the equipment. Then work on backing him up, then on moving his front end and his back end (see Chapter 4 for instructions on these three basic exercises).

These exercises are the foundation for working on a mounting problem. When you are reasonably competent with them, start using them to work on your issue. In the middle of the school, start on controlling his back end, then suggest that he stands still when you are facing his withers. Rub his withers with one hand and his back with your other. If he won't stand still, move his back end again, and ask again. Aim for having him stand still for a minute with you on each side of him.

What you do next depends on whether your horse is fearful of the mounting block or not. If he is, you need to attend to those feelings. Work him away from the mounting block (you can either lunge him or practice the three foundation exercises), then walk him around for a rest and lead him slowly and calmly past the mounting block. Repeat this sequence until you feel his anxiety lessen, then try standing him still there.

If your horse is not frightened of the block (or if you have worked with him to ensure that he is no longer frightened of it) repeat the exercise where you control the back end, and then stand him still next to you, but then take him to the mounting block for a rest. Keep repeating this sequence: move his back end – stand in the mounting position and rub him – take him to the mounting block for a rest. It is good if your mounting block is by a wall or a fence, so that the horse cannot get behind it.

When you're happy that the horse really knows this exercise, and he is calm and relaxed doing it, you are ready to start doing it at the mounting block. Stand on the mounting block and try to get him in the mounting position. If he will stand there, rub his withers and back as a reward, then get down from the block. If your horse is still a bit fizzy, work on the ground to move his back end, then stand still and rub. Repeat this a few times then try back by the block again.

If your horse will still not stand by the block, you might need to enlist the help of a friend. Start back in the middle of the arena, away from the mounting block. Hold the rope, but give your friend the stick. Imagine that you are a wall that the horse is tied to. Ask your friend to use the stick to move the horse towards you until he is in the mounting position then rub his withers and his back. You friend should also rub him with the stick. Do this on both sides. After a minimum of three good times on each side, repeat the exercise, but this time with you standing on the mounting block.

There is a slightly more advanced version of the moving the back end and rubbing sequence that you can use in combatting your mounting problems. In this version you stand in the same place, rather than moving with your horse. Start by standing at the horse's head, facing him while he stands still. Move his back end so that he swivels around sideways on to you, then rub his withers and back. Repeat this on the other side. When you have managed this exercise a minimum of three good times on each side over two days, try to do it with you standing on the mounting block.

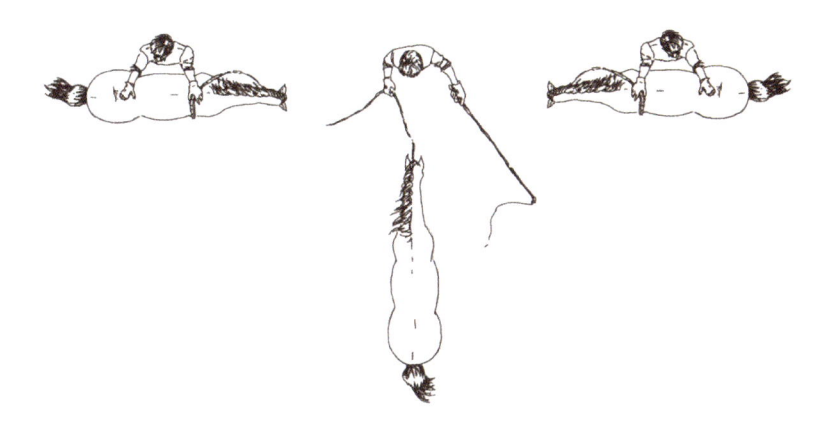

Some horses react better to the first exercise sequence, some to the second. But once you choose one, it will work if you believe it enough and repeat it enough. Follow your heart when choosing and you can't go wrong.

Leaning over your horse

After you have had at least three good times on each day for a minimum of three days doing the in-hand exercises with you standing on the mounting block, you can progress to leaning over your horse. Do plenty of in-hand work away from the mounting block, then bring him to the block to rest. Stand on the mounting block and carefully lean over him, rubbing him at the same time.

If you've had three good days of leaning over him bareback, you can think about saddling him up. Repeat the sequence of doing ground work away from the mounting block, then bringing him there for a rest while you lean over his back. When you have had some successes at leaning, you can start just putting your foot in the stirrup. Again, do these exercises from both sides. Your horse should be comfortable with being mounted from the left or the right.

If you have a portable mounting block, now try moving it to some different locations while you do this exercise. You should do this in as many places as possible. Your horse should be able to cope with this in the yard, in two or three places in the arena, in the field, and any other places that you can think of. You should also be able to try standing on different objects, such as a bale of straw.

Getting back on

If you have been getting good results in more than two locations, with the saddle on and putting your foot in the stirrup, then you can start actually getting on him. With all the preparation work you have done, this should be a big non-event for your horse, but you should still take it easy. As soon as you are on board, rub his withers, and have him stand still for a while. Sometimes just ride to the middle of the arena, sometimes take him out for a ride. There is no end to how often or for how long you should do these exercises. The only one who can really tell you is your horse. Observe your horse's reactions and his expectations when you do the exercises, and when you mount him, and you'll have your answer. If you feel any fear in him, then you need to repeat the exercises. If you feel that your horse is fed up with being ridden, then you need to introduce some more psychology balance to his life.

You should also be able to mount your horse from the ground, because you never know when you might need to do it (although using a mounting block is much better for his back). Start by getting the horse to stand still next to you and then put one foot in the stirrup. Rub him if he continues to stand still. A lot of horses will move as soon as you hold the reins and put a foot in the stirrup. If he does move, you need to move his back end away from you again while you are holding the reins. Release the reins and rub when he moves his back end away. Repeat this a few times until he will stand still while you grab the reins in the mounting position, then try putting your foot in the stirrup again. You also need to learn how to back your horse up using the reins. Hold the reins in two hands as you would if you were riding him, and back him up by applying pressure to the bit. Release when he steps back. This gives you another tool to help you when you are mounting from the ground.

As well as mounting from the ground, you should also be able to mount your horse from both sides. This is true whether you are getting on from the ground or from the mounting block.

If your horse is fresh, and moves off as soon as you get on him, you should bend his head towards your foot and ride him in a tiny circle to each side, and then suggest that he stands still. When he's still, get off, and get on him again until the horse stands still when you mount, happy, calm and safe.

Whenever you are mounting remember that your horse should feel that you are the leader. Take your time and don't rush. Move his back end a few times, maybe put your foot in the stirrup and take it out.

With most mounting problems I work with, I can generally get on and off the horse from both sides after about half an hour of working with him. But if the horse has had traumatic issues arising from being mounted, then I am prepared to take much longer with him, and it could take up to ten days. I wouldn't expect you to be able to learn all these new skills and use them with your horse within 30 minutes, your training plan should stretch over several days. With a horse that has had a traumatic experience, your training plan would cover weeks.

Even when you feel you have solved your mounting issues, you should plan some maintenance work. Some days tack him up as if you were going to ride him, but do some ground work with him instead. Adopt the mounting position a few times, and then continue with the ground work. At the end of your session, get on him and stand still for a minute, maybe even feed him a treat. You are giving your horse a stronger reason to be good the next time that you ride. Always train and work for tomorrow.

Chapter 11
The Lazy Horse

All horses can be energetic. Even if you think you own the most lazy horse on earth, you've probably watched him running around in the field with his friends and thought 'why can't he move like that for me?' Horses are born to move, and generally they like to move, but do they have a reason to move when we ask them to do it? When we ask a lazy horse to keep moving round and round the same arena, what's in it for him? If this horse loses the feeling that there's a reason to move, then the problems begin.

If we can understand our horses better and see what they are looking for then everything will start to change for the better. You need to show a lazy horse that you can be his trusted leader, and that you will be fair with him. On the one hand, he needs to see you as his best friend, whom he can rely on to keep him safe. On the other hand, you must be a 'bossy' friend: when you want something he knows he has to give it to you. The best and easiest thing for your horse should be to listen to you, so that he chooses to listen to you and you do not have to force him.

You might doubt that this is possible. Can you really make him happily cooperate without forcing him? The answer is yes, but the key is patience. Don't be in too much of a rush for the result, and don't get angry when you are adding pressure. You must give your horse a chance to understand what it is you're looking for, and timing is all-important. All the time a horse is not complying, keep your pressure up. The moment he gives you what you want, you must release the pressure, and that is his reward.

How did your horse get to be so lazy?

How does a horse become lazier and lazier? How come he stops feeling it when we kick him on, or when we use the whip? The best technique that a lazy horse employs is to tire his rider. When the rider is tired, they release the pressure and the horse has found his place of comfort without expending too much energy! (Being lazy, he prefers standing still to running away.) Imagine a rider repeatedly kicking her horse to get him to trot and getting no response; she stops when she's tired to have a breather before she starts again, but the horse still hasn't trotted.

Sound familiar? Have you been there with your lazy horse? But every time you do this your horse learns that the pressure you're giving doesn't really mean anything, and if they ignore it you will stop.

It's important for us to realise that every time we start to use pressure on our horse and release it before we've got what we want, we are increasing the problem. The next time we ask we will need to apply that pressure for even longer, or to use greater pressure, to have any chance of making the horse listen and comply.

Remember that horses are ready to learn all the time from everything that they see or hear. So if you start asking your horse to do something, you must understand the pressure rules really well. Make sure you are ready to keep up the same pressure until you get a result and, crucially, you can release the pressure at the right time.

Reasons to listen

Here are some of the reasons you can give a lazy horse to listen to his rider:

1. It is safer and easier for him to be with you than to be anywhere else. So ask yourself these questions:

    - Does he feel safe to go where you are asking him to go?
    - Is there a danger you are asking him to pass?
    - Can you protect him?

2. He wants to feel comfort and ease. A lazy horse is looking to do as little as possible, or to use the least amount of energy possible; so he might ask himself if he will be given a rest if he listens to his rider, or will they just keep asking him to do things anyway? Is there a difference between when he listens to his rider and when he ignores them? For example, if you kick him to ask for trot, and he does trot, will you just keep kicking him anyway? The lazy horse is often waiting for the ride to finish from the moment you get on him, but you can change this attitude with the right training. Always finish your training in the right place. Stop when they have given you something, when you feel that they would give you more.

3. He needs to understand and respect the power that his leader has. If we don't have the right power used in the right way with the right timing, our chance of a lazy horse listening to us is much smaller. When you ask a lazy horse to do anything, his first thought is to test how serious you are about the request by seeing if you will stop when he uses his 'tiring' technique. If you don't tire and don't cease your pressure, he will listen, but then will test how fair you are. If you keep up the pressure, even though he did what you asked, he will stop listening again. You need to teach him that the shortest way to finish a ride is to listen from the beginning. The most amazing thing about this is that when the horse decides to listen from the beginning he will start to enjoy it and the whole relationship gets better. Just ask a little bit more each time, and stop while your horse still has energy. You must keep the psychology balance right: work and reward. Remember that with lazy horses it's very easy to get tired by putting all your effort into the pressure. We can't be stronger than the horse, but we can be smarter, and more patient. Be very careful where you employ pressure D if you can't maintain pressure D!

4. Food. This sounds like a good idea, but isn't recommended with the 'lazy horse' personality. Keep it as a reward at the end of a successful session rather than as a tool in the training. Don't come to rely on it.

5. Herd and home. Most lazy horses want to return to their home and to their friends, knowing this will help you understand their behaviour.

Training the lazy horse

After you've studied and understood the points above, and have a better idea about how your lazy horse thinks and what he's looking for, you can start the journey to improving your relationship. The most important thing at this stage is to keep your immediate goals realistic. Do not ask for too much at one time, don't run the risk of not being able to keep up your pressure and teaching him the wrong lesson.

If your plan is to make him trot or to make him trot out, or even to make him canter, then trotting and cantering has to be a comfort place for him. There are worse things for him than going faster!

You also need to have a good understanding of what pressure and release means and how you are going to use them on your horse. You will be squeezing your legs against his side to ask for some more forward motion. But be careful not to ask for more than you can maintain, and don't increase the pressure, keep it constant. As soon as you get any forward movement, release your legs. This way the horse learns what you want, that you are serious, and that you have infinite patience. You can use a whip if you need to, but again don't use it with more force than you can maintain. Squeeze your legs for three seconds, if he doesn't move forward, keep your legs on at the same pressure, but add a gentle tap, tap, tap with the whip.

Again, as soon as you get any forward movement release the legs and stop the tapping.

How can we put this plan into action?

- First they must learn to move off your legs. At the beginning even getting a walk when you ask is good enough (at this point you don't have to worry about where they are going so long as they move forward).

- When you get them to trot, initially be happy with a trot. Don't worry about how good or how fast or whether your horse is 'on the bit', any trot is good. Ask for walk again quite quickly, so that it's your idea rather than his. Just keep repeating the transitions walk to trot, trot to walk. Don't rush, stay in this stage for two to four weeks. Remember that you are working for tomorrow. Sometimes it feels like you are getting nowhere, but you are getting somewhere.

- Gradually increase the length of the trot when you and your horse are ready. If he feels like he appreciates being brought back to walk, but does pick up a trot within about two seconds of you asking him, you can start increasing the length of time that you are asking him to trot for. Still just concentrate on getting a trot, don't worry about the quality of it yet, just now you want to teach him to keep trotting until he hears differently.

- If you are finding it easy to maintain your horse in trot, and he doesn't go back to walk without your asking, you can start thinking about asking for a faster trot. Up to now you've been working on controlling gait (walk or trot). Now you are starting to work on controlling speed. In this exercise slow trot becomes the comfortable place that walk previously was. Alternate between slow trot and faster trot. Use the same technique as you did earlier: only ask for short bursts of faster trot, and make sure that it's your idea to slow down.

- When you feel that your horse is viewing slow trot as the comfort place, you can go up another gear. Now start working on faster trot being the comfort place, and asking for short bursts of canter. Always remember that all these steps only work if you are patient, if you rush you are much less likely to succeed. If your horse has been happy in the fast trot for a minimum of 3-7 days in a row then you can start working on canter as a comfort place for your horse. Make your horse canter a bit faster each time he is lazy in the canter, and wanting to go back to trot, until you get to a point where your horse is happily cantering.

- If you have completed all the steps above and your horse is happy to be in all the different gaits and speeds, you can start to work more on speed control and collection, taking your horse's weight back on his hocks and his energy up or forward.

If you have got this far you'll understand, maybe for the first time, that the journey is way more important than the goals. All the time you've spent understanding how your horse thinks and how you can give him a reason to listen to you is the main thing. I really wish you a lovely journey, and I want you to start understanding your horse. No one on earth can ever be a better teacher than your own horse!

Chapter 12
The Horse with No Brakes

Do you have problems with your horse's brakes, does he ignore your 'slow down' commands to the point that you feel run away with? So how do you stop a horse who really doesn't want to stop?

Before you start to work on this problem, you need to ask yourself how much pressure you have on the reins when you are riding? Is there more pressure than you need? Many people hang on to their reins too tightly. This might be because they've been taught to ride with a heavy 'contact', or because they are scared that their horse will run off with them. Generally the faster they are going, the harder they hold.

But when you ride your horse while holding on tight, you are teaching him to ignore your pressure and go forward anyway. Some horses get to learn that an increased contact means 'hey, we're going for a canter' and react accordingly. You can't then expect to stop him by adding a bit more to that pressure. When you want to go forward, you shouldn't be exerting more pressure on his mouth than it would take to break off a blade of grass. Get a friend to hold your bridle by the bit and experiment with the pressure that holding the reins gives, then swap over and feel it for yourself. You need this light pressure while you want your horse to go forward in any pace: walk, trot, or canter.

You also need to think carefully about your timing when you try to slow your horse. If your horse responds, you should release the pressure straight away. Be particularly careful that you don't release and then immediately pull again, even if you're shortening your reins. But if your horse does not respond, or takes a long time to respond, then you need to do something about it. If you do nothing, the problem will only get worse, the horse will get stronger and it might take minutes to stop rather than seconds. A trained horse should slow down or stop within two to three seconds when you apply pressure on the reins.

The major tool that you need to use in resolving the 'no brakes' issue is teaching your horse to back up. Whenever you ask him to stop, and he doesn't obey within two to three seconds, you ask him to back up.

Backing up is an important part of any horse's education. It is not about making him go backwards as such, but rather teaching the horse to move away from pressure, and be respectful of it. When you pull lightly on the reins, your horse should go backwards. If your horse does not respect this pressure, then he will only stop when he feels like it. If something scares him, you haven't got much hope of stopping at all!

To change and to improve, you need to start with ground work. You're going to follow this sequence:

1. Work with backing him up in a halter
2. Work with backing him up in long reins attached to your halter
3. Work with backing him up in long reins attached to a bridle

Start teaching him to stop and go, and then back up. With the halter on him, walk by his shoulder. When you want him to stop, put some pressure through the rope onto his nose, as soon as he stops release the pressure. After he's stood still for about five seconds, agitate the rope to put pressure on his nose to make him back up. Again, as soon as he obeys, release the pressure. This exercise is both about him learning to listen to your pressure, and about you practicing your timing. Never put on more pressure than you can maintain. If he does not react straight away, you must be able to keep the pressure up until he complies – this might extend to minutes, not seconds! Your aim is to have him backing up within two to three seconds of you applying pressure. Work up to have him back around 10-20 steps.

When you have mastered this exercise in the halter, progress to using the long reins. Start by walking behind him (at a safe distance!), and repeat the exercise that you perfected with the halter and rope: walk – stop – back up. When you have him obediently backing up for 10-20 steps, the next day you can progress to trot. Run if you like! But you can also arrange your long reins so that you can stand in the middle of a circle, and 'lunge' him rather than run along behind him. Position yourself so you are level with his hindquarters (rather than his shoulders). Initially the inside rein goes directly to your hand, but the outside rein travels along his side and around his backside to your hand. If you have a roller, pass the rein through a side loop to stop it falling. A saddle will work equally well: tie your stirrups together using a rope passed under his belly, and route the rein through the outside stirrup. Work in one direction, and then swap over and work on the other rein. When your horse is used to long reining, you can thread the inside rein through roller or stirrup too (then you can change direction without having to stop and reconfigure your gear).

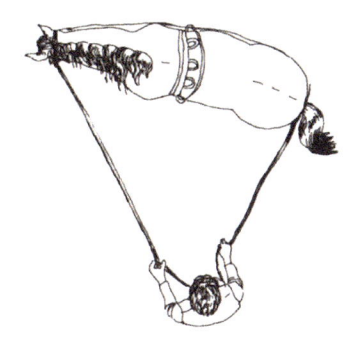

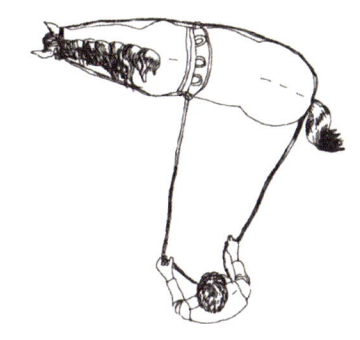

When you have mastered the use of the long reins tied to the side of your halter, you can start using your bridle, and attaching the long reins to your bit.

Aim to reach a good seven times in a row, with the horse stopping within about two seconds. Whenever it takes longer than two seconds, have him back up for you. He has to back up whenever there is a delay in him listening to your pressure. You are always working for the future: when you back him up, you are not punishing him, you are looking to make the horse more reactive to your pressure, and much softer in the mouth.

When you have seven good days working in trot like this, you can start performing the exercise in canter, again working up to having seven good days in a row. When you get to the stage where you can do this exercise in all three paces, and your horse is listening to you well, you are ready to get on him.

Start your ridden work in an area where you horse is comfortable, and feels both calm and confident. Immediately you get on him, try flexing his head to the left and the right, and riding in a small circle. Also just use your reins to back him up a few times. If you're happy that your horse is listening to you, start work on the exercises that you did on the ground, but this time with you in the saddle. The ground work that you did was preparation, it was not the cure, you might still encounter some difficulties.

Start your ridden work in walk. Repeat the walk – stop – back up exercise until you have three good days in a row. When you feel confident that he is listening, repeat the work in trot. Now you must have seven good days in a row before you start cantering. With the canter, start on a 20 metre circle and with just a few strides. Canter a quarter circle, stop and back up. Then work up to half a circle, stop and back up. When you are happy with that, canter an entire circle.

When your horse is really good on the circle on both reins, try the same exercise in a straight line. Start with walk and trot, and when you're confident he's listening, progress to canter. Now you are ready to go out for a hack and try the exercises out on the trail or bridleway. Practice getting your horse listening to you both when you ride him alone, and when you ride him with other horses.

Starting to compete again

If you've suffered the indignity of brake failure while you've been out competing your horse, you will want to test your new controls before you compete again. Try going to a different arena or field in another yard and work through your exercises. If you can, take your horse to an event two or three times before you actually enter. Just lead him or ride him around the ground and test out your brakes in that atmosphere before you put the pair of you under the pressure of actually competing. If you have two or three OK times with this, then you might think of actually entering a competition. When you do enter, concentrate on the experience, not on winning (actually, the less you think about winning the more likely you are to win).

Chapter 13
The Horse who won't Load

Difficulty in loading a horse into a trailer or lorry is very common. It is the most common problem that I am asked to deal with. Most horses can be persuaded to load in their first training session, but that is really only the beginning of the process of setting them right. Be prepared to take a long time if you want to transform your horse to an easy loader, and a happy traveller.

Some horses flatly refuse to go anyway near a ramp. Some load just fine, but throw a fit as soon as the ramp goes up. With any of these issues, you should first take some time to figure out why your horse does not want to load, or why he travels really badly.

- Maybe he is a complete beginner and has never loaded or travelled before. In some ways this is the easiest case to deal with, but you are doing your horse a big favour by taking it slowly and following this plan. (You are also doing yourself a big favour, because there is every chance you will avoid the travelling problems that other horse owners have.)

- Maybe your horse became difficult after some incident that occurred while he was travelling. This might be an accident, bad driving, or even being bullied by the horse he was travelling with. Whatever it was, it has really put your horse off the whole idea of getting in a box and going somewhere.

- Maybe you have a lazy horse, and he knows that loading in a box means going somewhere where hard work will be expected. Equally it might be the journey itself that he's not looking forward to. Keeping your balance in a trailer or lorry while travelling a long distance can be pretty hard work for a horse. (Generally, this type of horse is just fine once he is on board.)

- Maybe sometime in your horse's past he was really bullied into loading. Once he was in, the ramp was quickly shut behind him and he was driven off. This type of horse will shoot out again as soon as you arrive at your destination, which can be quite dangerous. His experience taught him not to trust, because he feels like he was punished for cooperating. This case can be the most difficult to fix.

Remember that loading and standing happily in a box are two different things, and you might need to work on both of them. You will also need to work on unloading safely.

There are two main techniques for loading a horse, sending the horse forward into the box, or leading the horse from the front. It is better to start with sending the horse forward, because this method is safer for you (no chance of you being squashed between anxious horse and breast bar, for example).

You can help your horse with travelling confidence by getting him used to standing still in one place, where he can't see his friends and has no food to distract him. Every horse should be able to be tied up like this for a minimum of half an hour.

Before you get anywhere near a trailer or lorry with your horse, you must teach your horse some basics first, to make sure that he is listening to you really well.

- He needs to know the 'something/nothing' exercise
- He needs to back up to your command

- He needs to be 'light' behind the ears (obedient to the halter)

Work on guiding your horse from the side. Start from his left side, holding the rope in your left hand and the stick in your right hand, so that you are slightly turned towards him. He should walk with you by his shoulder. You use your stick or string to guide him gently forwards. If he turns his head towards you (most horses will) bring your stick across your body, and hold the string while you tap his nose to keep him straight. Use pressure on the nose from the halter to make him back up. Work on this technique, repeating walk – stop – back up. Swap to the other rein, so that you are standing by his right side, with the rope in your right hand and the stick in your left hand and repeat the exercise. Aim for a minimum of seven good times in a row on each side. If you are not in a rush, repeat this exercise so that you have a good three days.

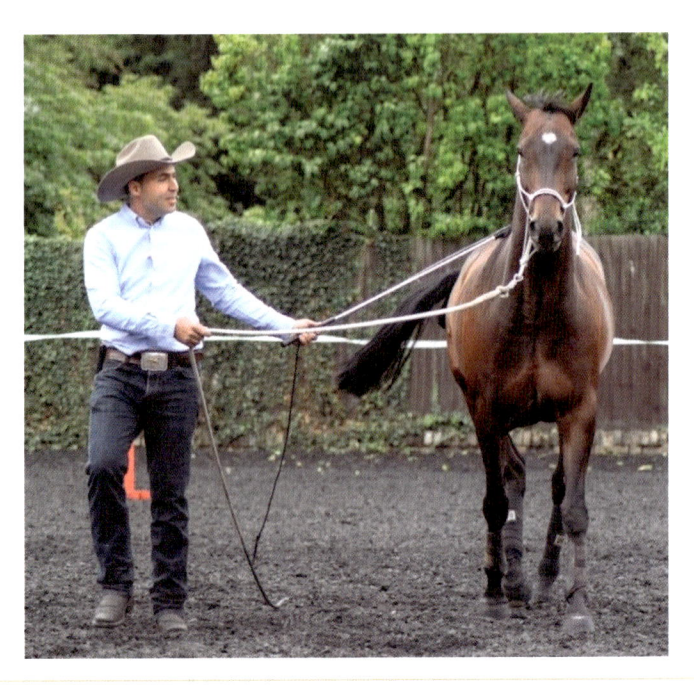

The next stage is to find some sort of obstacle to make your horse walk across. This could be a tarpaulin, some rubber matting, anything that could represent a trailer or lorry ramp. You now need to have a similar conversation with your horse as you had before, sending him across the obstacle, and backing him up. The obstacle is standing in for the ramp. You are getting your horse in 'listening mode', and viewing you as his leader which is a necessary forerunner to you loading him.

After you have accustomed him to the obstacle, work on your horse's straightness. Use a cone, or similar object, and put it in the middle at one end of your obstacle (if you haven't got a cone, you can use a two litre plastic drink bottle, filled with earth or sand to weigh it down). You are going to use the cone as a target. You have to send your horse in a straight line towards the cone, with his back end not drifting to one side or the other. Keep repeating this and correcting him until he's straight; you can trot as well as walk if you like. Aim for seven good times in a row. Then see if your horse will reach forward and touch the cone with his nose – some will do this naturally, some might need more encouragement.

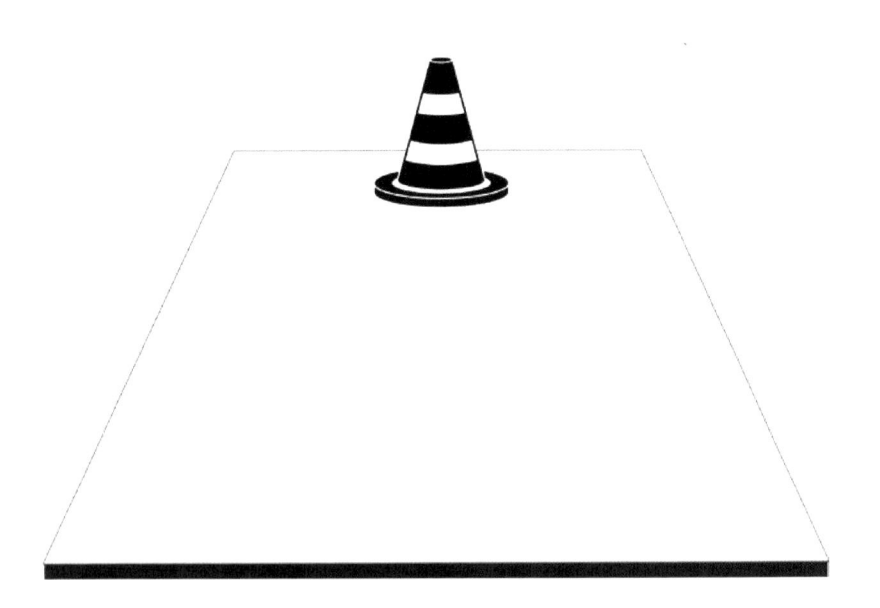

Now you are ready to start working with the vehicle that you actually want to load your horse into. Try and park the trailer or lorry somewhere where the ground is soft and not slippery (concrete is the worst surface!) At first just lead him up to the ramp. Visualise your cone on the ramp and aim for straightness. You should have at least three good ramp approaches in a row with a fairly relaxed horse before you progress to letting him put his nose on the ramp a few times. Then get him to put his front feet on the ramp, stand still, and then back up. Repeat that for seven good times in a row. Each time you take your horse away from the ramp, you are building his trust and confidence, which greatly increases your chance of success. If you are not in a hurry, then leave it there until the next day (remember that the more desperate and rushed you are, the more frightened your horse is likely to be).

Whenever you continue, the next step is to get all four feet on the ramp, and then back up. Repeat this for three to seven times. Many horses will try to sniff the side of the ramp at this stage. This is not necessarily a bad thing, so long as they are trying to sniff their way into the box, rather than sniff their way out of it. You can judge this by where they are sniffing. If, after you have all four feet on the ramp, you feel that the horse wants to go further, encourage him. The horse might even offer to walk in, which is the best way of achieving your end results.

Whenever the horse wants to back up, be more than ready to let him. But don't let him stay there and get comfort, send him forward again straight away. The idea of letting him back is to show him that there is a way out and build his confidence (don't we all feel safer when we know the way out?) Timing is everything in this situation; when the horse wants to go backwards put no pressure on him until all four feet are off the ramp, and then put the pressure on again. It is very important that you do not get angry if your horse backs up. Just imagine you are saying to him 'you can stay out if you want to but I will keep right on tapping you with this stick'. A lot of horses will run out or turn and jump off the ramp. Keep calm – just reposition and put on pressure until they put their feet back on the ramp. Remember to use only the level of pressure that you can maintain, and prepare – above all – to be patient.

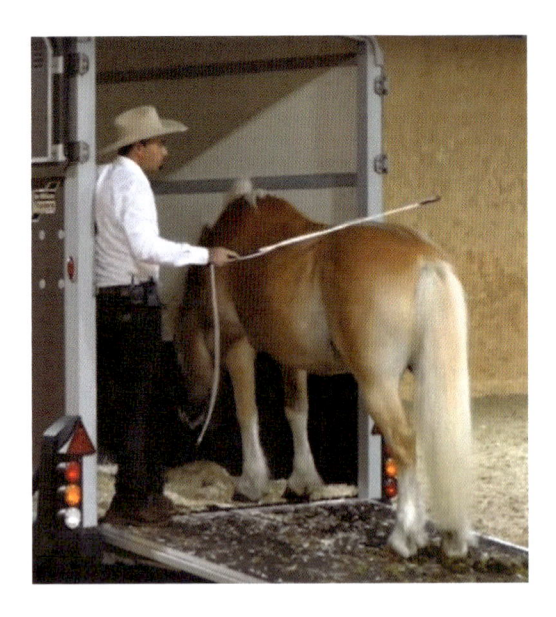

When you get to the stage where your horse will go in, bring him out straight away. Do not shut the ramp behind him or put the breeching bar up. Aim for seven good times in a row, with your horse being calm about it. Then you can start increasing the time he spends inside. Start with 10 seconds, then increase to 20 seconds, then to 30 and so on. When you reach 10 – 15 minutes with a horse happily standing in the box, you can do up the breeching bar and close the ramp, and then tie up your horse. You need at least three good days in a row before you actually travel him anywhere; seven days would be even better. Let him stand in the box, relaxed with a haynet, for around 30 minutes before you actually drive off.

Choose as straight and easy a route as you can for your first journey, and leave plenty of time for the trip, so that you're not feeling rushed or stressed. Maybe you are taking him somewhere different, but you could equally just take him for a drive around and then back to your yard. Whatever your destination, when you get there do not unload your horse straight away. Leave him standing there for 15 minutes at least, or for as long as it takes him to stand there calmly. This could be half an hour, an hour, even up to two hours. When you do unload him, load him again straight away, and unload him when he's calm again. When your horse has been able to cope with loading, travelling, and unloading without getting upset for a few times, you can start on your seven breaks. Use the breaks to work out how often you need to load and travel your horse to maintain his new skill. For most horses this will be every month or every couple of months for the first year or two. After that, he should feel confident and be able to oblige whenever you want to take him somewhere.

Chapter 14
The horse that bucks

Bucking is very common among the problems that horse owners are likely to encounter. Accordingly, this is about the longest chapter in this book! There are five main reasons that a horse may be bucking when you ride him, and your first task is to identify which one applies to your horse, so that you can follow the correct plan for curing him.

Read on to help you work out which of these five reasons causes your horse to buck:

- Laziness
- Confusion
- Fear
- Excitement
- Energy

Reason 1 – laziness

This might sound counter intuitive – why would a lazy horse put energy into bucking? But a lazy and dominant horse can work out that if he bucks every time you try to canter him, you might just give up cantering him! This is just about the most common cause of bucking. So, if you have a horse that tends to buck as soon as you ask for a faster pace, once you have ruled out health-related issues such as bad back or saddle fit problems, you should proceed with this plan.

Start with ground work. Work on the lunge and then on long reins to be able to move your horse's feet through all the gaits smoothly and nicely in both directions. Aim for a minimum of seven good days in a row. You can then go on to work using your reins as if you're riding, but standing at your horse's shoulder. Work on walk/trot and trot/canter transitions; you can use your whip in the same way as you would if you were on board.

You start on the ground because it is easier, smoother and safer. You need to aim to have your 'slow' as good as your 'go'. Working on your 'slow' gives your horse a soft mouth, which in turn helps keep you safe. You can keep your horse's head up easily if he tries to buck, and a horse can't put in a serious buck without putting his head down. Use the backing up exercises to work on your horse's softness.

When you have progressed with your ground work, you can get on your horse. Your main task here is to work on transitions. Aim to have two speeds at walk, and three speeds at trot, and the ability to stop and back up. With any of this, don't progress to a faster pace before you have three good days in the slower one. If your horse does buck at any point, you need to be ready to keep your horse uncomfortable. Use your legs or your whip, and use them in rhythm, but without any anger. As soon as the horse moves forward, release the pressure. Use a bit of psychology balance here: make him go forward in the pace that you asked for for about ten seconds, but then let him go slower for at least another ten seconds as a reward. Work up to spending a minute at the desired speed.

If you have three good days in a row working in trot, you can move on to canter. This is the most common gait for having bucking problems, but you should feel confident that you'll probably solve this problem quicker than you expect having done all the preparation work in walk and trot. The first time that you ask for canter you must prepare yourself to be persistent. Once you ask for a canter you cannot release the pressure until you get one. Remember that there is absolutely no room for anger – do not take your horse's behaviour as a personal insult. Five to ten strides of canter will do at first; release the pressure as soon as he canters and then let him back to walk after a few strides. You need to keep repeating this exercise until you get three good times in a row with no bucking. Don't stay in canter for too long, just keep repeating canter – walk, canter - walk.

On your next training day, repeat the canter, walk, canter, walk exercise, but increase the distance that you canter. If you previously had ten strides, go up to 15 or 20 strides. Also increase your requirement to seven good times in a row. Not all horses will maintain improvement from the first day; on the second day you might find that they are even more determined to test you, but keep up the exercises and believe that they will improve.

Keep at it until you get three good days in a row, that is, three days with no bucking when you ask for canter. At this point you should employ a bit of psychology balance. On the fourth day, take the horse into the arena and just walk and trot – introduce a few strides of canter at the very end of the session, no more than ten, and then stop and get off. On day five, put more fun into your training. Place two barrels in your arena and put some carrots on top. Canter between the barrels and let your horse eat a carrot every now and then. (If you have a very greedy horse, you might need to enlist a friend to act as a carrot custodian.)

On the sixth day get back to some more serious work. Ask the horse to stay longer in the canter. Always be ready to go back to use psychology balance to encourage your horse and to give him safety and comfort.

Reason 2 – confusion

A horse can buck because he is confused and impatient. He doesn't want to put the effort into working out what you want. This horse hasn't been trained to search for comfort by offering positive behaviour to his rider. Take a step back and start working on your horse's reaction when he's unsure or confused about what you're asking for.

Start on the ground and plan to build his patience and get him to offer you a positive action when he's confused rather than a negative one. The more we fill our horse's brain with new exercises and new things to offer us, the more patient they will be when we ask them questions. If all your horse knows is left/right/stop/go, that is not enough. Your problems might manifest themselves when you ask for something like leg yield in trot. He doesn't understand – he's tried getting faster, but that didn't work, so he gives up and bucks. If you want to teach your horse to keep offering you positive actions until he gets the one you're looking for, you stand a better chance with teaching him new things.

On the ground, you want him to master a big list of exercises:

- Sideways away from you
- Sideways towards you
- How to move front end
- How to move back end
- How to control his speed

Chop and change a lot while you are working through these exercises. For example, move sideways from the edge of the school towards the centre, then interrupt this and get your horse to move forwards. Then resume the sideways movement again. Repeat the transitions between walk/sideways to forward trot. The key is to ask for frequent changes.

When I'm training a horse like this and I feel that he is watching my body language, and I can ask him to stop in the middle of any gait, then I will ask him to just stand still for about three minutes. Why do this? Because with impatient horses you want to make sure that they can be still when they're expecting to be asked to move their feet. When you reach the stage that the horse can perform transitions with you leading from the side, moving sideways and then forwards, and can stand still for three minutes a minimum of five times in each session, and you have had three good days in a row, then he's ready for you to get on board and continue with the training.

Start the next session with a bit of preliminary ground work, and then mount your horse. You can then continue with building your leadership from the saddle. Build on it gradually. This type of horse often doesn't have a problem with forward movement – they are not usually lazy. This problem is most likely to turn up in horses that are confident and energetic (though you might find it in horses with different personality types).

Use similar exercises in the saddle as you used on the ground. It might also be good to teach him how to stop on one rein by bending his head towards your knee. Practice riding him in a tight circle on each rein. Then try stopping him at walk then at trot by pulling his head round to your knee. If he doesn't stop straightaway keep him circling until he does stop, then release and rub him as a reward. Repeat on both reins and repeat until you get three good days in a row. This adds one more positive thing for him to suggest to you when he's confused. This horse learns that there are different ways of behaving to regain his comfort if he doesn't understand, rather than just bucking.

bending the horse

You might need the help of a friend to teach your horse to go sideways while you are riding him. Make sure your friend is able to move him sideways using the in-hand aids before you get on. After you've mounted, get your friend to move your horse sideways, while you give the ridden aids. Repeat this until you can move sideways on your own. When you've mastered this, perform similar transition exercises to the ones that you did on the ground. For example, try moving him sideways and then transition to canter him forwards. Follow a sequence like move sideways to left –> canter forwards a few strides –> move sideways to right –> canter forward a few strides.

Always be ready to keep your horse uncomfortable until he complies. But be careful about how much pressure you add when he bucks, don't add too much, just keep going and continue asking. Above all, keep training with transitions.

Reason 3 – fear

Bucking from fear can be the worst, and the most dangerous, cause. If your horse bucks when he's frightened as a way of protecting himself, you can have quite a journey to resolve this problem. You need to start by figuring out where his fear is focussed when he acts like this. Is he frightened of something above him while being ridden? It could be your clothes, your balance, voices, too much movement in the saddle, if you drop something, the list goes on and on. Sometimes it might be the surrounding environment that he has problems with and it's nothing to do with his rider.

If, whenever you are about to mount, you see your horse lift his neck higher and become wide-eyed with fear then you know that the source of his fear is something happening above him. He might just hold himself tense and stand still for you, but really the horse is a bit of an unexploded bomb: he's an accident waiting to happen. If you see these signs, then I'd really recommend that you don't ride this horse until you've addressed his problems. The good news is that I've helped many horses like this, and many are now very good horses (my quarter horse, Sandy, is an example of such a horse). Be prepared to take your time though, there is no quick fix for this problem.

Start on the ground with a lot of 'something and nothing' exercises. You are going back to the basics and your aim is to add many more things that your horse regards as a 'nothing' rather than a 'something'. He must start to learn that lots of the things above him and around him can safely be ignored.

Begin with the most basic 'something and nothing' of rubbing him all over with your stick. Then throw the string over his back from both sides. Progress to leading him from the side while rubbing him with the stick over the top of the back: hold the rope in your outside hand and the stick in your inside hand. Try doing this in trot as well as in walk. Keep in the same gait until you feel that he's really calm about the rubbing. After you have thee good days in a row, you can make thinks a bit more challenging by using a small flag, or a bit of plastic bag tied to a stick (avoid the colour white to begin with, it can be too alarming). The first part of this exercise is to get the horse to sniff the flag and follow it along the ground. When he is happy to follow and sniff, then carefully try to rub him on the neck and shoulders with the flag. If he tries to run, be more than ready to keep at it until he accepts it. When he does, rub him and release. Keep repeating until you have three good times on each side. And then build up until you have three good days in a row when you can rub him all over his body.

Now you can repeat the exercise where you led the horse from the side in walk and trot, but this time hold the flag above his back where the rider would be and occasionally touch him with it. When you have three good days in a row with this exercise, change to using a larger flag, or plastic bag. The bigger the flappy object that your horse can cope with, the safer he will be. Introduce some umbrellas as well, and put jackets and other objects on the ground. Every time that you increase the challenge, work to have three good days in a row.

Once your horse is happily coping with all that, take the horse and stand him next to your mounting block (a place where you previously saw him to be tense and scared). Rub him with the scary objects while he is standing by the block, and work up to seven good days in a row doing this. Use some psychology balance when you're doing this, if he's relaxed by the block, let him eat some food from it (but don't use the food as a way to get him calm).

There is still more work to do with this horse before you actually get on him. You need to start long reining him, and when you're both comfortable with that, start adding some obstacles in. Get him to pass a tarpaulin on the ground, pass between two open umbrellas, and so on. Ask a friend to take the flag and stick and wave it above his back. Aim for three good days in a row with your long reining exercises.

Now it is time to start riding your horse. If your bucking problem was caused by fear, then there is a good chance that you have already solved it with your ground work.

Hopefully you'll get on and find that you have a different horse underneath you. At first remove all the obstacles from your arena and concentrate on increasing your control in go and slow for three days. Then start reintroducing the scary objects on the ground. If your horse is 100% with these, then ask for your friend to come and rub the horse with the flag while you're in the saddle. Now try some transitions from walk to trot between the umbrellas. It's also a good idea to change training areas at this point. Maybe go to the corner of the field, or to another arena. When you do this, start with in-hand work, and then do some long reining before you actually get on.

Reason 4 – excitement

The horse that bucks through excitement might have a strong instinct towards his herd and his home. He might be impeccably behaved – positively angelic – when he is at home. But when he is out for a hack he can become very worked up about getting home again. This horse might get particularly excited when he sees other horses going somewhere, and might want to run to them. He can be cross because a horse leaves him, or because he's away from the yard on his own. If you feel he's going too fast in his mission to get home, or to be with other horses he's seen, you might well find that he bucks when you try to slow him down. Some buck a little, some buck quite a lot.

You have to work out what the main cause of his excitement is. Is it caused by other horses, either horses leaving him or horses in the distance? If this is the case, you will need some help from other riders. Start with ground work. Ask a friend with a horse to ride around you both in trot and in canter until you can continue to lead your horse in walk and trot. Your friend should pass you in a straight line while you continue in a straight line. Your horse must stay calm while moving and while standing still for a minimum of three good days in a row, then you can think about mounting them.

Repeat these exercises while you are riding, with the same horse and rider helping you out. Circle round them, and have them circle round you. Pass each other riding straight lines, then ride next to each other and include transitions of walk, trot, stop and back up. When your horse has been good for a few days, you can try cantering, but be careful not to rush this stage.

This type of horse is often challenging to turn out, and this work can help you with this as well. When turning him out, add in some psychology balance. Take him towards the field, but turn back, go in and out several times. This way he doesn't know whether he's going to be free or not. Take his headcollar off and let him go when he isn't expecting it. Take some carrots or other food and let him be eating when you release him. Use more carrots to encourage him to stay even after he's free.

You will need to take this horse inside the herd field and lead him around while his companions go about their horsey business – eating, rolling, running and so on. Keep your horse concentrating on ground work while this is going on. When you have a minimum of three good days without him being excited, this is a sign that he's ready to be ridden out (any earlier than this can be dangerous). Ask the same friend that worked with you initially to accompany you on a hack (pick a friend whose horse is calm and sensible when out, otherwise you are better off going on your own).

When you're out, find a nice open space and go through some of the same exercises. When you are ready, ride in the herd field as well, while the other horses are present. With this, as with so much of Shady Horsemanship training, the idea is not to wait until terrible things happen, but to 'cover your future' by training horses to get them used to anything they might have to face on a ride. You are developing your ability to tell your horse to slow down and change his mindset when he gets excited. The bucking problem should have disappeared by now. Keep you horse busy before he keeps you busy. Keep changing direction and moving in small circles to the left and to the right. The more he sees you as his leader, the less he cares about anything else in the environment.

Reason 5 – bucking from energy

You need to distinguish the energetic bucker from the overexcited one. If your horse has an energetic personality and he tends to buck when you ask him to slow down, you are most likely to be dealing with this problem. To work with this issue, you need to sort out and balance your horse's energy. Do this by doing lots of training and keeping him busy.

Most of this training will be ridden, but you might benefit from doing some ground work with him before you ride him; take some energy out of him before you get on. But you are working on teaching the horse to keep his energy, so that eventually you should be able to just get on and ride.

Your horse most likely trots when you want him to walk, and bucks when you won't let him canter. Above all else, this type of horse has to learn to respect the reins. This will involve lots of stop and back up transitions. Start to make a change by using different transitions. Begin with these:

Walk -> stop -> back up
Trot -> stop -> back up

Build up the amount that you let them go forward gradually. Start with two steps, stand and back up, then ten steps, stand and back up, up to 14 steps, stand and back up. Backing up teaches your horse to respect the reins, but it also holds his energy back, and stops him going too far forward. You should feel him beginning to wait for the sign to go back.

After you have had three good days with these transitions, you are ready to ask for more: to start riding transitions in canter. Canter your horse for a few strides then try to bring him back to trot. He should slow within two seconds, if he takes longer then make him back up. These transitions teach a horse to respect your rein and respond much quicker, but be aware that it won't teach your horse to maintain the gait that you're looking for. If you are trotting, but your horse keeps going into canter, you don't have to back up provided that he listens to your reins and comes back to trot within two seconds. You're giving him pressure when he canters, and release when he trots, so he should be able to figure out what you want. If he does take too long to respond, don't be afraid to stop him and back him up. Through respect for the reins, you should be able to maintain the pace you're looking for.

Chapter 15
The horse that rears

Rearing can be a very frightening problem, and just as with other issues, you need to begin by working out what is at the root of your rearing problem. There are three possible reasons why a horse might stand up with you:

- Dominance
- Confusion
- Fear

Reason 1 – rearing to express dominance

The dominant horse rears every time he's asked to do something he really doesn't like doing, or to enter a place that he doesn't want to go. He might rear to get away from anything he doesn't like, even something like sponging his neck. This behaviour gives him the comfort that he's been seeking, it's his way of not doing what the leader wants.

You can work out if dominance is the cause of your rearing problem (rather than fear or confusion) by observing when your horse does it. Always be on the lookout for signs of fear, but if your horse is a bit lazy and he tends to rear when you ask him to go forward, even into a place that he's familiar with, then the chances are that he is testing you. If you give him a release when he rears then he will carry right on rearing whenever you ask him to do something that he doesn't want to do.

To deal with this problem you need to start with ground work. You need to work on leading your horse in the guiding position (hold the rope in your outside hand and your stick in the inside hand). Perform walk/trot/stop/backwards transitions, and work through any rearing behaviour that you get. Aim for a minimum of three good days in a row leading from both sides. Then start adding some obstacles that your horse might refuse to go over, for example, a tarpaulin on the ground. You are not doing this to make your horse have this experience, as you might do with a nervous horse, for example, you are doing it to build more trust and respect. More importantly, you are creating a situation where the horse might rear to get away. Instead of waiting for it to happen, you are making it happen, having already made the preparations for dealing with it. By now you have the minimum of the tools and the horse language you need. You'll have learned to use the stick with a good tapping rhythm on his back to keep him uncomfortable and under pressure, without hurting him and, above all else, without you getting angry. Always remember that you love your horse, it's his behaviour that you have the problem with, and you can fix that.

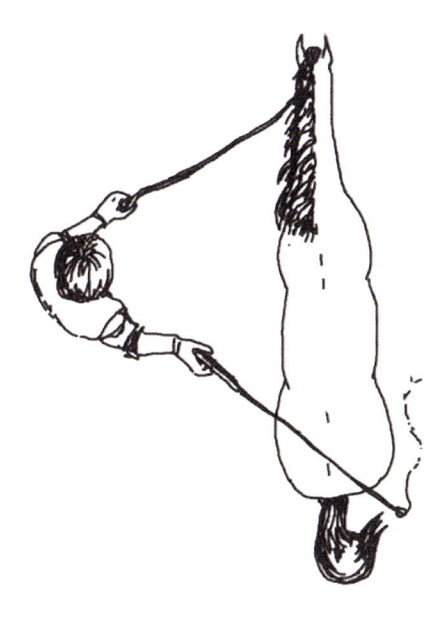

the guiding position

When you are ready, with the tarpaulin in place, start tapping your horse to go towards it. The first thing you want is for your horse to go and sniff it. If he is already rearing, you have to keep the pressure on until he faces it, then release and rub, and back him up six or seven steps. Go forward again to the same spot, and repeat this three to seven times. Each time, take a few more steps forward until you reach the point where your horse is happy to put his nose on the tarpaulin and sniff it. Then you can ask your horse to put his front feet on it, and work up to him walking over it. If he rears, back up, then come forward again keeping the pressure on until you get to the point where he misbehaved, and then release. Give him a five second break standing there, and ask him to move forwards again. Keep repeating this until he realises that rearing isn't going to bring him relief.

Normally, the horse will take the decision to walk over the tarpaulin. Most horses will rush over it at first. If this happens, just keep repeating the exercise until he slows down. Now think about your environment, and places where you can take him to practice this work: places that he has previously reared to avoid. Practice your new skills, see if you can get him between, underneath, and over objects he has objected to. The more that you are in the situation where you can turn a big 'no' into a 'yes' the more chance you'll have to solve this issue when you get on board, after all it is the same horse with the same brain! Once he's got used to listening to you rather than rearing, he should be able to transfer this behaviour from ground work to ridden work.

A good halfway house is to transfer from ground work to long reining. Make sure that you have good transitions between walk, trot, stop and back up. Then ask him to walk over the tarpaulin, and deal with the other obstacles that you used when you were working him in hand. You could add taking him in and out of the yard, especially if one of his tricks was to rear whenever you asked him to leave his home.

When you have a minimum of three good days with this long reining work, then it is time to start riding again. You should feel much safer in that you are much more prepared to deal with any problems. The first exercise when you're on top is to practice bending your horse's head round to your knee (you might try bending his head on the ground first). Most horses cannot rear (or buck) when they are in that position, especially if the rider does not hesitate to maintain a full bend. By doing this you are continuing to build communication and respect and also developing a tool to deal with a rear should it happen. Each time you detect that your horse is thinking about rearing, take his mind somewhere else, for example, by bending the neck. Try circling to the left and then to the right with a bent neck. Also try giving away your reins. With a dominant horse, especially one that is also lazy, the longer the reins, the less likely they are to rear. Concentrate on getting them to move forward and avoid putting pressure on the bit. At this stage of your training you're working on the basics, don't worry about riding in a contact or asking for an outline. You want your horse to understand that he needs to move forward off your leg, introducing more quality into that movement can come later.

The exercises that you should work on when riding is for your horse to know go and slow, forwards and backwards really well. Some people might tell you that backing up makes a horse rear, but really learning to back up on demand will only improve your horse.

One thing to be aware of is the timing of your release. If you ask the horse to move forward and he rears, you want to ask for forward again as soon as his front feet are back on the ground. You must approach this with 100% confidence. Be ready for him to rear up as many times as he likes. When the horse is up, you don't need to add any pressure, just lean forward and put zero pressure using legs and hands until he arrives back on the ground. At that moment you should ask for forwards, bend his neck round, or ask for backwards (whichever you feel most comfortable with). Bending or backwards are most likely to help you survive this experience, do not give up on your horse, and do **not** give him release until he complies. Then your horse has not won, and a lot of the time just repeating this sequence will solve the problem once and for all. Just remember that timing is crucial, put the pressure on when all four feet are on the ground.

Are you worried that your horse might go over backwards with you? Normally, they will not do this if you release when they stand up (and are less likely to do this if you've done your groundwork well). I can say that in the last fifteen years, this has never happened to me, even though I generally deal with at least one rearing problem per week.

Reason 2 – rearing because of confusion

A horse that rears when he's confused is a horse that doesn't want to put the effort in to understand his leader. He would rather rear if he doesn't understand. This is different to bucking through confusion, and tends to happen with a particular type of dominant horse. Having said that, the exercises you need to deal with this problem are quite similar to the exercises for dealing with a horse that bucks through confusion. The big difference that you need to make is to increase this horse's patience. This type of horse is often impatient even when he's tied up. You'll see him pawing the ground, or even rearing to get away, he might well be a head shaker too.

Again you need to start on the ground. You are aiming to get him to give you positive action when he's confused rather than a negative one. Use the same exercises as for the horse that bucks through confusion and impatience:

- Move sideways away from you
- Move sideways towards you
- Move the front end
- Move the back end
- Control his speed

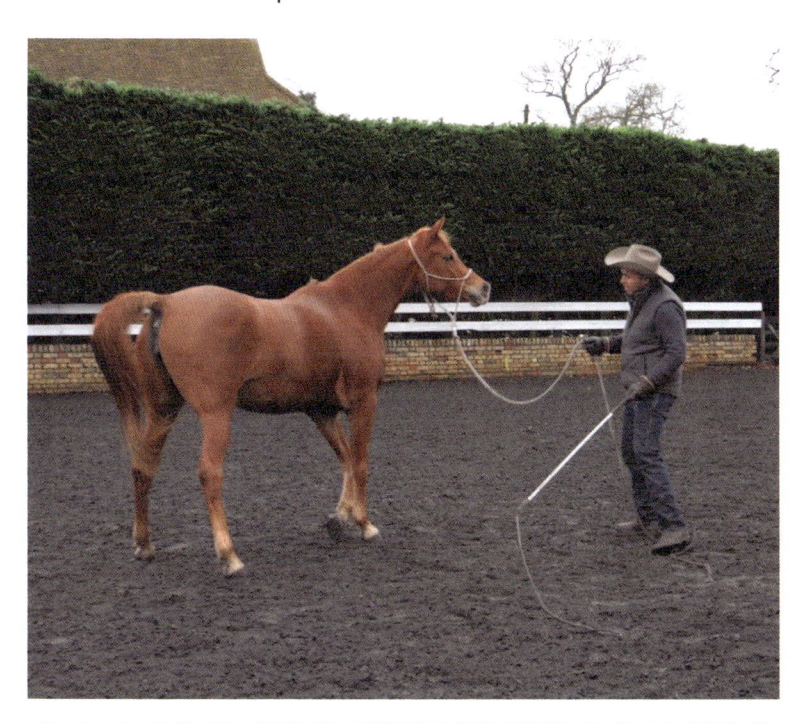

Cycle between these exercises quite quickly, performing lots of transitions. The sequence where you start moving a horse sideways, then ask him to go forward, then back to sideways, is a particularly useful exercise. Add in a figure of eight, making him stop and back up while he's doing it. Each time your horse is unsure, he will show this by rearing. Your job is to keep the pressure on and then release and rub when you get what you want. Repeat these exercises and teach him some more (see the section on the horse that bucks through confusion for more ideas). A good indication that you're succeeding in changing his mindset is that you'll be able to tie him up without him fidgeting or rearing.

Now it's time to start riding him. Use similar exercises in the saddle as you taught him on the ground. Again, look at the chapter on confused bucking for detailed instructions on how to repeat these exercises in the saddle.

Reason 3 – the horse that rears through fear

When a horse is scared of something they won't normally rear unless they can't get away from the thing they're scared of, or they're being made to go somewhere they are frightened of. You can recognise fear in this horse by looking for signs such as a raised neck, wide eyes, tense body and so on. You might not even be aware of what is scaring your horse. We could write about the many reasons why a horse might be scared, but this would fill another two books. You can look at the chapter about spooky horses to get some ideas about recognising signs and causes of equine fear. Always be mindful of a horse's instinct for herd and home. There are many horses that rear from fear because they already lack confidence due to being taken away from their companions. They are already tense and worried, so many good horses can turn into dangerous horses because they think they can't cope without their friends. The first step with these horses is to increase their confidence on the ground.

You can use the same exercises for the scared horse as have been recommended for the dominant horse in the first section of this chapter. Use the same obstacles, but concentrate on building the horse's trust and confidence as he negotiates them. Add more obstacles, and have more friends helping on the ground. After you have worked with the obstacles in hand, start using the long reins.

With a horse that is scared, you have to take a softer approach. If a horse takes one more step towards an object that he is scared of, reward him by taking him away from that object. That way you are building his trust and confidence in you, and expanding his comfort zone. If you are walking him and he suddenly freezes, take this opportunity to work out what it is that has made him freeze. Wait a while until you see his tension release before putting pressure on him to take him forward again but just for one or two steps. You can work him in a figure of eight pattern to take him towards and away from the feared object. All rearers should have a good go and a good slow, and be good at bending their heads and following the reins before you think about getting on them.

After you've had a good seven days in a row on the long reins, and feel that your horse is much more able to cope with his fear, taking confidence from you, then you can get on him. Then work through the same exercises with the same obstacles as you did in hand and with the long reins.

Chapter 16
The horse that bolts

There's a difference between brake failure and bolting. Bolting is sudden and unexpected, rather than a horse that just wants to go faster and you're having trouble pulling up. Everything has a reason and there are two main reasons why horses bolt. One is fear: they see something that alarms them so much they ignore their rider and run away from it. The other is dominance, a horse knowing that it can get away from what you've been asking by running. A bolt can start out as a fear response and end up as a dominance response. The dominant horse will often head for home if out on a hack, or for the gate if working in the arena.

The dominant horse

You have to make the dominant horse respect your reins really, really well. They must react whenever you pull on them. Backing up is a crucial skill in this process, and you need to get to the point where the horse will back up in response to the lightest of rein pressure. You want to teach your horse to back up in three different speeds: dead slow, medium, and almost running backwards. You also need decent transitions:

Trot -> stop -> back up
Fast trot -> stop -> back up
Canter -> stop -> back up

You can start practicing these transitions on the long reins, and then continue in the saddle. These are the tools that you need to deal with this problem, but you also need to think about the underlying reasons why your horse is behaving like this. Try and introduce some psychology balance to help fix it. For example, if your horse bolts to the arena gate, give him reasons to like other areas of the arena and to associate the gate with work rather than relief. Start riding small figures of eight near the gate: bend your horse's neck to the left and to the right and practice having him follow the reins. Many horses won't follow the reins properly and need to be taught how. Don't give them release until they follow the rein with their shoulder and their front feet. If they try to run at this point, focus on what you want, not on what might happen, and maintain or increase the rein pressure until they follow it. Do not release the rein, or switch to the other rein to turn them the other way. Getting a horse into a particular place is much less important than getting him to follow your rein. You must only release the pressure when the horse complies, otherwise you are teaching them to ignore your reins and run. You must not lose your faith: believe that it can end in a positive way, otherwise you might release your pressure because you are scared.

Exercise this horse by the arena entrance, and then take him to the middle of the arena and let him rest. Carry on with this until he feels happy in all parts of the arena. Add more psychology balance by keeping him guessing when your session has ended. Ride him out of the arena, and then ride him back in again (you might need the help of a friend to open and shut the gate). Try leaving your arena and going to a field to carry on with your training. Keep repeating this for seven days in a row. He won't know what the arena means, or what outside the arena means, and you no longer feel him drawn to the arena exit.

If you have been doing your arena training with a closed gate, now do it with an open gate. Start with ground work, lead or long rein him past the open gate to and fro in both directions. You can add in some food rewards if you like. After you have three good days in a row you can get on him again. Add some more psychology balance: place a few buckets in the arena, containing carrots or similar treats. Prepare as if you are taking him to the arena for a work session, but then walk him around and let him enjoy some snacks. If you can, take him out of the arena to do some work elsewhere, then ride him back in for more snacks. Introduce a session like this every so often.

At this stage of the training be very aware of the pressure you have to use on the reins. He must have 100% respect for your reins. Remember that if you ask him to slow down or stop he must respond within two seconds. You must not release rein pressure until he's responded to it, whatever has happened. It makes no difference if your reins are different lengths, you've lost a stirrup or whatever: what is important is the amount of pressure going to the mouth, it must be the same or more until the horse has responded. In this situation, faith is all-important once more. Do not lose your belief when you are having a difficult conversation with your horse. I have never seen a horse stay in a place where he is uncomfortable, but I have seen many riders release at the wrong time and lose confidence, or start with more pressure than they can maintain.

The fearful horse

This horse is different to the dominant horse, but you need to start the training in the same way: in the saddle in a safe place working on respect for your reins. Like the dominant horse, you must work on transitions and aim for your horse being light in his mouth. Once your horse is prepared and ready – following your reins nicely to the left and right – then you can start on the journey of building your horse's trust and confidence. You want to arrive at the place where, if your horse is scared and wants to run, he listens to you when you put pressure in the reins and say 'no, it's all fine'.

Start this journey by finding out the things he's really scared of, and work on swapping his reaction of running away to a reaction of standing still and thinking. Most horses like this are scared of things behind them, and they want to run away from them. You need to work on changing their reactions to one where they think standing still is a better answer for their fear. Start on the ground with a flag or a plastic bag on a stick. Don't put it behind the horse straight away, start with pulling it along the ground in front of them and encouraging them to put their nose on it and sniff. Then try rubbing the horse with the flag. If he runs keep hold of him and keep the flag on him, when he stands still, take it off and give him relief. The intended lesson is that if he stands, the fearful thing will go away, whereas if he runs, it will follow him. As he gets used to this, move to using the flag behind him and repeat the exercise. Have someone follow the horse with the flag until he learns to stand still. You can repeat these exercises with a number of objects (see the chapter on bucking for some more ideas).

If your horse reacts badly to certain sounds, then you can try a similar exercise of exposing your horse to the feared stimulus and encouraging him to stand still. Download or record some examples of the feared noise and play it over some speakers. Start with a low volume, but turn the noise off only when your horse is relaxed and calm and stands still. Resume and turn the volume up slightly. Aim for the point where the horse can hear the noise but just ignores it, a sign that it has become a 'nothing' in his mind. Horses must learn to ignore many things in their life, and the more they learn to ignore, the better it is.

You can take your work of exposing and re-educating your horse outside the arena too. Say your horse is very reactive to rustling in the hedge, enlist the help of some friends, and even some well-trained dogs, to expose your horse to these stimuli and build his confidence in dealing with them. If you get the help of friends with this, they must commit to helping you until you get three good days in a row with this type of training. Aiming to follow the 7-7-7 formula will make your horse even more secure, but bear in mind this might mean your friends helping you for around 20 sessions!

The emergency stop

With any horse that bolts, no matter what the reason, you want to feel confident that you can stop them if the worst does happen. Add the one-rein stop to your training. Teach your horse to stop when you use one rein to pull his neck to the left or to the right. Get yourself and your horse used to this technique in the school environment. If your horse takes off with you, and you want to use the one-rein stop, take the decision and pull one rein straight away. Don't start pulling with both reins and release the pressure to pull one rein. If you want to be safe, try to not to let fear and 'what if's' enter your mind. Stick to a plan of pulling both reins, or pulling one rein until the horse stops. Believe that your horse will stop if you pull constantly without hesitating.

Enjoy your training journey!

Printed in Great Britain
by Amazon